CASTRO!
CASTRO!
CASTRO!
CASTRO!
CASTRO!
CASTRO!

DON E. BEYER

An Impact Biography
Franklin Watts
New York Chicago London Toronto Sydney

FOR MY FATHER, MARVIN M. BEYER

Photographs copyright ©: AP/Wide World Photos: pp. 1, 2 bottom, 3, 4, 7, 8, 9, 10, 13 top, 15; UPI/Bettmann Newsphotos: pp. 2 top, 6 inset, 11 top; Archive Photos, NYC: pp. 5, 6, 11 bottom, 12, 14; Miami Herald Publications: pp. 13 bottom (John Pineda), 16 top (Maurice Cohn Band); Reuters/Bettmann Newsphotos: p. 16 bottom.

Library of Congress Cataloging-in-Publication Data

Beyer, Don E.
Castro! / Don E. Beyer,
p.   cm. — (Impact biography)
Includes bibliographical references and index.
Summary: Documents the life of Cuba's charismatic leader, from his early days as a revolutionary to the present, and examines his economic and social reforms.
ISBN 0-531-13027-4
1. Castro, Fidel, 1927–   —Juvenile literature.   2. Cuba—
Politics and government—1959–   —Juvenile literature.   3. Heads of state—Cuba—Biography—Juvenile literature.   [1. Castro, Fidel, 1927–   .   2. Heads of state.]   I. Title.
F1788.22.C3B49   1993
972.9106'4'092—dc20
[B]   92-34534 CIP AC

CONTENTS

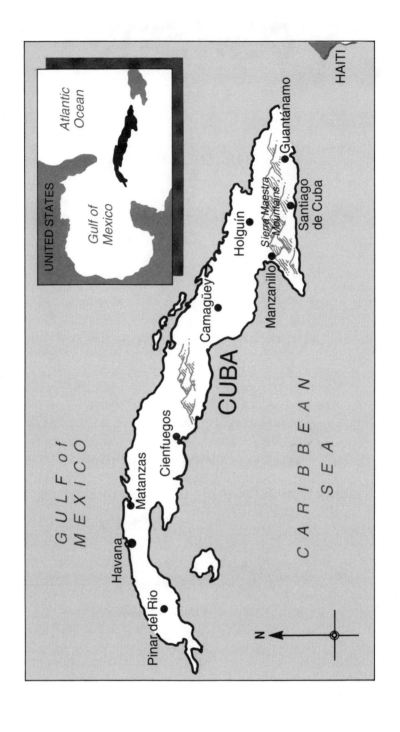

CHAPTER ONE

ENTER
THE
FIGHTER

Fidel Castro is a man at odds with the world. He likes to say that he came into it under conditions natural for a guerrilla fighter. He was born on August 13, 1926, as an explosive storm swept over the mountains of Oriente Province, the wild land that has long served as an incubator of revolution in Cuba.

Fidel Alejandro Castro Ruz, one of seven children from two marriages, was born illegitimate, as were other of his brothers and sisters.[1] His father, Angel Castro, and his mother, Lina Ruz González, were not married until some years after Fidel's birth. Lina, Angel's second wife and twenty-five years his junior, came to the Castro household as a teenage maid. When Angel's first wife, María Louisa Argota, could no longer ignore her husband's affair with this girl, she divorced him and left the area.[2]

Both Fidel's parents were of Spanish descent, with roots going back to that area of Spain known as Galacia. Angel (full name Angel María Bautista Castro Arguiz) was born in Spain to a poor peasant family on December 8, 1875. At age twenty he joined the army and a few years later, in 1898, went to Cuba to soldier during the short-lived Spanish-American War.

By the time of Angel's introduction to Cuba, the island had been a Spanish possession for four centuries, ever since Christopher Columbus had claimed it for Spain on his famous voyage of 1492. Cuba, known as the "Pearl of the Antilles," was prized for its strategic placement within the Caribbean world. It served as the base for Spain's New World exploration. In the late eighteenth century, Cuba's prosperity and its nearness to the newly conceived United States of America attracted considerable U.S. interest. There was even talk of annexation.

By the late nineteenth century, U.S. business interests in Cuba, especially those connected to the sugar industry, had greatly expanded. Spain objected to this growing influence but could do little to prevent it. Nor could it stamp out the desire of many Cubans for freedom from Spanish control.

Demands for independence led to the Ten Years' War (1868–1878) and the War of Independence (1895–1898). Officially, the United States remained neutral in these conflicts; unofficially, many Americans sympathized with the independence movement and would have been pleased to see Spain ousted from its last holdings in the Americas.

Matters came to a head in February 1898 when an explosion ripped through the U.S. battleship *Maine* as it lay at anchor in Havana harbor. Though the cause of the explosion was never determined, the U.S. press blamed Spain and managed to inflame public opinion. The *Maine* incident, plus long-standing hostility toward Spain and growing concern over the

protection of business interests, led the U.S. government to demand Spain's withdrawal from the island.
War soon followed and was soon over as weak Spanish forces proved no match for the power of the U.S.
Navy. Cuba became independent but was occupied
as a protectorate of the United States. Spanish soldiers in Cuba, among them Angel Castro, returned
home. But having experienced the green richness
of Cuba, Angel saw little future for himself in the
windswept poverty of Galacia. He soon returned to
the island and, in time, settled in Oriente Province
to seek his fortune.

Angel started with the American-owned United
Fruit Company as a poor day laborer. After some
time working as a peddler catering to the needs of
local sugarcane cutters and woodsmen, he organized
his own workers and leased their labor to United
Fruit. In one of the few times he ever spoke publicly
of his father, Fidel called him "a very active, enter-
prising person" with "an instinctive sense of organization."[3]

Angel bought and leased land which he forged
into a sugarcane and cattle empire covering 26,000
acres. He became a very wealthy man during the
great sugar boom following World War I. Despite his
money, Angel never rose far above his peasant roots
and remained the hard and violent man he had had
to be to wrest an estate out of virgin forest. He was
the model for many of the behaviors and attitudes
Fidel would come to exhibit: the drive for power and
control, a disdain for democratic forms of government, the tendency to be a law unto himself, and
a hostility toward the United States of America—
usually referred to contemptuously as the "Yankees."

Lina Ruz, Fidel's mother, also came from humble
beginnings. Early in the century she and her family

had relocated to Oriente from the Pinar del Río province of western Cuba, traveling more than 620 miles (over 1,000 km) by oxcart. The poor and unschooled young servant girl who caught the eye of Angel Castro stayed on to become the mistress of the estate.

The Castro family estate, the ranch or *finca* on which Fidel Castro grew up, was a rough and ready country place in the municipality of Birán. There was no town, just a collection of a few buildings lining a dirt road a long way from anywhere. Near the Castro house squatted a bakery, a tiny elementary school, a general store owned by Angel, and a post and telegraph office. The area was too poor and unpopulated to support a church, one reason Fidel was not baptized until the age of six when he attended school in Santiago.

Early in the development of the *finca*, Fidel's family lived in a rough wooden house on stilts, built by Angel in the manner of houses he had known in Galacia. At first, animals sheltered under the house. When the family became more prosperous, a separate barn was constructed nearby.

The frontier conditions of the *finca*, far from the influence of cities, suited Fidel, an intelligent boy consumed by energy and easily bored. He loved and was at home in the outdoors, something he carried with him as a revolutionary in the Sierra Maestra mountains and later as the ruler of a country. In his growing-up years in Birán, he climbed its hills, swam its rivers, and hunted its wild lands with horse, dog, and gun. The rugged land was the ideal setting in which a boy might freely indulge his passion for physical activity.

Fidel's unconventional family life, the tumult of a large family in an unrestrained environment, forced him early into independence. His father, busy being powerful and rich in a poor country, had little time for close relations with his children. He was as bad tempered as Fidel grew to be, and their relationship through Fidel's youth was distant, unloving, and often hostile.

Fidel has spoken little of his mother, Lina. Their relationship was apparently an affectionate one. She is remembered as a gun-toting woman who managed the family store, rode the ranch on horseback, and signaled the dinner hour to her dispersed family by firing a few shots into the air. Those dinners, in keeping with a loose family structure, were often taken with the family members standing up, a habit Fidel reverted to often in his adult life, to the wonder of many of his associates.

The wealth of the Castro family was enough to enable it to rise in society. Yet the opportunity for achieving social status on the frontier was limited. In later life, Fidel the revolutionary became defensive about his parents' wealth. He sought to avoid any suggestion that his roots were aristocratic or even upper middle class. A champion of the lower classes, as he wished to present himself, needed suitably lower-class roots to gain credibility. Fidel never liked to think of himself as being the beneficiary of a privileged upbringing. Nevertheless, he was.

Fidel's formative years lacked the traditional anchors of Cuban life: strong family bonds and an upbringing in the Catholic Church. Perhaps as a result, the young Fidel was often wild and uncontrollable. He went into frequent violent rages, produced legendary temper tantrums to get his own way, and defied authority at every turn.

Fidel began his formal education at the local school near his house in Birán. He was four years old. By all accounts, including his own, he was a very difficult child whose behavior was only tolerated because of his family's important position.

I spent most of my time being fresh. . . . I remember that whenever I disagreed with something the teacher said to me, or whenever I got mad, I would swear at her and immediately leave school, running as fast as I could. . . . One day, I had just sworn at the teacher and was racing down to the rear corridor. I took a leap and landed on a board from a guava-jelly box with a nail in it. As I fell, the nail stuck in my tongue. When I got back home my mother said to me: "God punished you for swearing at the teacher." I didn't have the slightest doubt that it was really true.[4]

Because of the boy's disruptive behavior at the local school, his parents sent him to a more disciplined environment in Santiago, the capital of Oriente Province. Quite possibly his father could not stand to have him around. The decision put its mark on Fidel.

It was a frightening thing for a little boy, only four-and-a-half or five years old, to be torn from the security of his mother and home in the country and sent to the strange new world of the city. Fidel recalled many years later, "I remember that I wet the bed on the first night."[5] Fidel's distress at being displaced increased because of his unhappiness as a boarder with the family of his former teacher in Birán. Angel and Lina seem not to have understood his distress or that the money for his support was being misused. He was neglected because the family was poor. His loneliness in Santiago may have lessened a bit when he was joined there by a sister and brother, but it also meant that his host family had more mouths to feed. Little of the money paid by Angel for board went for food. Fidel recalled in a 1985 interview with Brazilian priest Frei Betto:

We got a small container with a little rice, some beans, sweet potatoes, plantains, and things like that. The container arrived at noon, and it was shared first by five and then by six people, for lunch and dinner. I used to think I had a huge appetite: the food always seemed delicious. Actually it was just that I was always hungry. It was a rough period.[6]

It was during this time that Fidel was baptized. Angel had originally intended that Fidel's namesake, a rich and powerful man by the name of Don Fidel Piño Santos, should serve as the child's godfather. This was not to be. Owing to the difficulty of getting godfather and priest together at the same time at the remote Castro *finca*, an early baptism never took place. Living in a setting where almost everyone was devoutly Catholic, Fidel suffered because of the delay.

... I remained unbaptized, and I remembered that people called me a Jew. They used to say, "He's a Jew." I was four or five and already being criticized, for people were saying I was a Jew. I didn't know the meaning of the word *Jew*, but there was no doubt that it had a negative connotation, that it was something disgraceful. It was all because I hadn't been baptized, and I wasn't really to blame for that.[7]

Finally, in Santiago, Fidel officially joined the Church. One of the women of his host family married Luis Hibbard, a consular official from Haiti, and the Hibbards became his godparents. With a sprinkle of water Fidel went from "Jew" to Christian and attained legitimacy in the eyes of a church he would never embrace.

Fidel's new status in the church little affected his life in Santiago. For the first years of his education in the city, he was tutored at home by his godmother, an unemployed piano teacher whom he remembered as "a good and noble person." He had no books, but learned basic arithmetic from the tables printed on the cover of his notebook and reading and writing from his godmother's dictation. It was a time of "un-met needs" and "hardship."

> I think I spent around two years there just wasting my time. The only useful aspect was the experience of tough, difficult conditions, hardships, and sacrifices. I think I was the victim of exploitation, in view of the income that family got from what my parents paid them.[8]

Fidel's formal schooling in Santiago began with his enrollment at the Colegio La Salle run by the Catholic Marist order. Fidel started as a day student, then became one of thirty boarders at about age seven. In third grade, he was joined at La Salle by his brothers Ramon and Raúl. None of them fared very well. Once Fidel got into a fistfight with a priest he accused of humiliating him. The three brothers received such bad reports—charges of bullying, cheating, and not studying—that Angel refused to return them to school after the fourth grade. The others didn't seem to mind, but Fidel must have decided that his future pointed toward Santiago. He tried to force his parents to return him to school.

> I remember going to mother and explaining that I wanted to go on studying; it wasn't fair not to let me go to school. I appealed to her and told her . . . that if I wasn't sent back, I'd set fire to the house. . . . So they decided to send me back. I'm not sure if they were afraid or just sorry for me, but my mother pleaded my case.[9]

Fidel returned, not to the La Salle school, but to the more prestigious Colegio Dolores of Santiago run by the Jesuit fathers, the men who were to have such a molding influence on his life. Over the next twelve years, Fidel received an education reserved only for the privileged. Not only was such exclusive private schooling beyond the reach of most Cubans, its form and content were uniquely Jesuit. It emphasized self-discipline, obedience to authority, eloquence in public speaking, and breadth of knowledge—all qualities Fidel was to deem important in his later life.

Fidel was a rebellious and combative student whose temperament seemed more suited to the battlefield than the classroom. Recalling the early years at Dolores, his brother Raúl remembered,

> He dominated the situation . . . every day he would fight. He had a very explosive character. He challenged the biggest and strongest ones, and when he was beaten, he started it all over again the next day. He would never quit.[10]

While at Dolores, Fidel wrote a fan letter to the president of the United States, Franklin D. Roosevelt. He apologized to Roosevelt for his fractured English and congratulated him for being "president of a new era." "If you like," he invited with typical Fidel audacity, "give me a ten dollars bill green american . . . because never, I have not seen a ten dollars bill green American and I would like to have one of them."[11] The White House responded with a letter thanking Fidel for his support. Roosevelt did not include the ten.

In time, Fidel modified his behavior in order to survive in the conservative and disciplined environment of the Jesuit school. He channeled much of his aggressive energy into an area of endeavor which welcomed and rewarded it—sports. Fidel became an accomplished athlete. He thrived on the competition, always needing someone to test himself against. His success in soccer, basketball, jai alai, baseball, and other games made him a popular sports hero.

Fidel's accomplishments in the classroom were not heroic, but he got along. He was able to maintain good grades by virtue of his photographic memory.

In a system geared to passing big, end-of-term examinations, he was able to coast along doing little work, then, at the last minute, use his wonderful memory to cram successfully for the test. He was the envy of his classmates. Sometimes he showed off to them by reciting word-for-word whole pages of a book he had just recently skimmed. In later years, Fidel's prodigious memory enabled him to give the impression of knowledge and competence where it did not exist. It contributed to the popular myth of Fidel as the all-wise guru.

Fidel's success in sports, his ability to memorize, and his willingness to moderate the more rebellious and rambunctious side of his personality in order to stay in school enabled him to succeed at Dolores. When he left school at fifteen, his teachers remembered him as one who was determined to excel and distinguish himself. The boy who expected the president of the United States to give him ten dollars also expected the doors of the future to open for him as he moved on to the next level of his education. "I consciously decided to seek new horizons," Fidel told Frei Betto. He persuaded his parents to send him to Havana.

Fidel was sixteen when he transferred to the Colegio de Belén, or College of Bethlehem, the most prestigious Jesuit school in Cuba and perhaps the best secondary school in the country. Located in a wealthy suburb of Havana, Belén catered to the cream of aristocratic and wealthy middle-class society. About a thousand students attended classes in its large, imposing buildings and expended youthful energy within its excellent sports facilities. The latter, rather than the classrooms, especially attracted Fidel Castro.

The basketball courts, the baseball and soccer fields, the track, and the swimming pool became the areas in which Fidel chose to make his mark. He was a passionate, aggressive athlete, consumed by the desire to win at all costs. Driving himself at the expense of his studies, he practiced incessantly, even insisting that the school authorities install lights on the outdoor basketball court so he could work out far into the night. Diligence and his strong sense of purpose turned Fidel into a star athlete. A yearbook picture shows a tall, lanky, and muscular Fidel passing a basketball with serious determination. The caption reads, "Fidel Castro, because of his love for the school and the enthusiasm with which he defended the Belén School colors in nearly all the official school sports, has been declared the best athlete of the term."

In his enthusiasm for the active life, Fidel joined Belén's Explorers, a Boy Scout–style group of seventy boys, which emphasized outdoor pursuits, physical discipline, and quasi-military organization, all of which appealed to his growing need for order and control. He soon rose to the leadership of the group. The Explorers made weekend excursions into the wild country of Cuba where they hiked, camped, and climbed mountains. Fidel thrived on the challenges and dangers of the outdoors, often displaying the physical courage he would exhibit in later life.

On one excursion recalled by his mentor and adult leader of the Explorers, Father Armando Llorente, Fidel and the father found themselves separated from the rest of the group by a dangerously flooded river. Fidel swam about 200 feet (60 m) across the torrent with a rope in his teeth. When his turn came to cross by holding the rope, Father Llorente stumbled and was in danger of being swept away. Fidel rushed back into the water to assist him. Safely back on shore, they both dropped to their knees in a prayer of thanks.

Fidel thrived on the athletic training and the adventurous outdoor excursions afforded by his time at Belén. In later life he believed that they foreshadowed his activities as a revolutionary in the rugged and wild mountain terrain of the Sierra Maestra. "I didn't know—nor could I have imagined then—that I was preparing myself for the revolutionary struggle." [12]

Devoting so much effort to athletics and outdoor pursuits left Fidel little time for his studies. He was never a particularly enthusiastic student and relied on his photographic memory to get him through his subjects at Belén just as he had at the Colegio Dolores. Father Llorente remembered him as a "good" student but not "deep." He was also lucky.

Students at Belén had to pass state examinations to earn nationally recognized academic qualifications. These were especially suited to Fidel's talents for intensive, eleventh-hour study sessions. But sometimes he got careless.

Because he had done virtually no work in French and logic during his last term, school officials suspended Fidel from attending these classes. This meant that he could not take the final school and state examinations and graduate with his class. Fidel cut a deal with his instructors. If they would allow him to take the state examinations, and if he achieved scores of 100 percent on both, he would be allowed to take the school examinations. Fidel crammed around the clock for three days. He scored 100 percent on the state examinations, then repeated the performance on the school exams. Intelligence, intensity, discipline, memory, and brashness served the schoolboy as they would the revolutionary and leader of a country.

Despite the efforts of his teachers, Fidel was not the student he might have been at Belén. Nor did he succumb to the religious indoctrination of the Jesuit fathers. He was never more than a nominal Catholic. The required daily attendance at mass and the countless repetition of "Hail Marys" and "Our Fathers" had little effect, except perhaps a negative one that turned him away from organized religion. He told Frei Betto:

> Nobody could instill religious faith in me through the mechanical, dogmatic, irrational methods that were employed. If somebody were to ask me when I held religious beliefs, I'd have to say: never, really. I never really held a religious belief or had religious faith. At school nobody ever managed to instill those values in me.[13]

Yet the environment of Colegio de Belén did leave its mark on the character of Fidel Castro. As contradictory as it may appear, his rebellious spirit and aggressive nature found a home in the conservative, disciplined, and orderly atmosphere of the Jesuit program. The Jesuits valued intelligence, obedience, honesty, courage, honor, and sacrifice—most of the same characteristics that Fidel came to value in himself. "The Jesuits," he told Frei Betto, "clearly influenced me with their strict organization, their discipline, and their values."[14]

It may also be that, enveloped in the Jesuit atmosphere of dedication and commitment to young people, Fidel experienced a sense of belonging, perhaps even of family, something he never experienced at home among his own family members. The school, despite its conservatism and strong discipline, gave him more of a place to be himself than did the restrictive and narrow confines of an isolated family life in Oriente Province.

Even Jesuit efficiency and order could not suppress the expression of Fidel's violent nature. His temper was a drawn sword to be used against anyone who dared to cross him. He fought often, though not always successfully or well. A fellow student, Ramon Mestre, once made the mistake of calling him "crazy." Fidel got the worst of the ensuing fistfight, bit Mestre on the arm, then ran to his room and returned with a pistol, which he used to bluster and threaten until it was taken away by one of the priests.

Fidel attended Belén during the last years of World War II and took a great interest in the strong men and dictators of the day. Fidel's political awareness was beginning, and he looked for heroes to emulate. He found their names on the lips of those around him and in the newspapers and speeches that echoed the events of a world at war.

From the politically reactionary Jesuit fathers, most of them Spanish and not Cuban, Fidel was exposed to the ideas and personalities of the Spanish fascists. These strong men—*caudillos* in Spanish—became personal heroes to the young man who aspired to be strong himself. The founder of the Spanish Fascist party, José Antonio Primo de Rivera, and the Spanish dictator, Francisco Franco, were the role models of his own Spanish heritage. Fascism's disdain for democracy, its emphasis on supreme order and control, its flashy uniforms and other trappings of military paraphernalia appealed to Fidel.

His admiration also encompassed the other famous fascists of the day, Adolf Hitler of Germany and Benito Mussolini of Italy. Fidel is remembered at Belén for walking around campus with a copy of Hitler's *Mein Kampf* under his arm and aping before a mirror the posturing and bombastic speeches of Mussolini. In time Fidel would also come to admire the strongmen of the political left. The qualities he admired in them—their vision of a new order, their charisma, their power to manipulate people with speeches and impose their will—were common to all successful dictators.

Fidel's serious political awakening and involvement would occur at university, a few years down the road. Now, in the spring of 1945, he was about to graduate from Belén. The caption under his picture in the yearbook would read, in the optimistic and best-foot-forward language typical of yearbooks,

Fidel distinguished himself always in all subjects related to letters. A top student and member of the congregation, he was also an outstanding athlete, always courageously and proudly defending the school's colors. He has won the admiration and affection of all. We are sure that, after his law studies, he will make a brilliant name for himself. Fidel has what it takes and will make something of his life.[15]

The proud words of Father Llorente were prophetic.

CHAPTER TWO

LAW
AND
REVOLUTIONARY
POLITICS

The University of Havana, like many universities of Latin America, had long been home to political activity and dissent. It was especially so in October 1945 when Fidel Castro came to Havana as a student of law. The university served as a caretaker of the revolutionary spirit that had arisen in Cuba in the late nineteenth century and fueled the fires of change into the twentieth.

Cuba's first outburst of revolutionary fervor began in Fidel's own Oriente Province in 1868. Carlos Manuel de Céspedes, dissatisfied with Cuba's colonial status, led other native Cuban landowners in a fight for independence from Spain. The ten years of violent and destructive conflict that followed failed to achieve that goal. Though Spain introduced reforms to dispel further interest in independence, a second revolutionary war broke out in 1895.

The guiding spirit of the Second War for Independence was Cuba's most beloved patriot, José Martí. Martí organized a revolutionary campaign from exile in the United States where he formed the Cuban Revolutionary Party. In early 1895, Martí landed in Oriente Province with a small group of followers and joined the revolutionary army under the leadership of generals Máximo Gómez and Antonio Maceo. When Martí was killed in battle a month later, the revolution lost its most important civilian leader and organizer and gained its most famous martyr for independence. In succeeding years, the spirit and words of Martí would be invoked by Cuban leaders to support a wide range of often conflicting political ideas. No one did this with greater skill and effect than Fidel Castro, who saw himself as Martí's spiritual heir.

Despite the loss of Martí, the guerrilla war raged on for three years, then ended as a result of U.S. intervention and the defeat of Spain in the Spanish-American War (1898). The war terminated Spanish control of Cuba but resulted in a three-year occupation of the island by U.S. military forces. The United States agreed to leave Cuba in 1901, but not until the U.S. Congress's Platt Amendment had been incorporated into the new Cuban constitution. The legislation ensured America's right to intervene in Cuban affairs whenever it deemed appropriate. Article III of the Platt Amendment stipulated:

> That the government of Cuba consents that the United States may exercise the right to intervene for the preservation of Cuban independence, the maintenance of a government adequate for the protection of life, property, and individual liberty, and for discharging the obligations with respect to Cuba imposed by the Treaty of Paris on the United States, now to be assumed and undertaken by the government of Cuba.[1]

Cuba gained nominal independence in 1902 but continued to be dominated politically and economically by the United States, which invoked the Platt Amendment to intervene in Cuban affairs in 1906–1909, 1912, and 1917. A U.S. naval base established at Guantánamo Bay on Cuba's southeast coast served as a sentinel for American interests. It remains so today, to the continuing annoyance of the Cuban government.

Following the U.S. exodus, Cuba suffered from a chronic case of bad government, highlighted by the corrupt and bloody dictatorship of Gerardo Machado (1928–1933). In reaction to Machado, revolution broke out in 1933 and expressed itself in acts of terrorism, political assassination, strikes, and mass demonstrations. A coalition of forces—elements of the middle class, the Communist party, and radical student groups—aided by U.S. pressure on Machado succeeded in his ouster. Carlos M. de Céspedes won the presidency but held it only briefly. A military coup led by an unknown army sergeant, Fulgencio Batista, unseated Céspedes in January 1934. Batista and his supporters created a revolutionary government headed by Ramón Grau San Martin. In the volatile political atmosphere, Grau's leadership lasted only a few months. His successors held little real political power, which, behind-the-scenes, remained in the hands of Batista and the military. In 1940, Batista achieved legitimacy by winning the presidency. Four years later he left office, obeying the no-direct-succession provision of the constitution. The presidency passed to Ramón Grau, who was in office in 1945 when Fidel entered the University of Havana. Fidel's first efforts as a political activist were aimed at the Grau regime.

The university was Fidel's laboratory, the place where his growing social and political awareness joined an expanding sense of self. After his twelve years of sheltered, privileged, and restrictive Jesuit education, the university offered a heady, free-thinking, liberal environment more suited to Fidel's natural temperament and ambition. Early on, he set out to make a name for himself.

The nineteen-year-old came to the university in style. He had money in his pocket and drove a new American car, courtesy of Papa Castro. It was never clear, even to Fidel, why he chose the study of law. One needed to choose something. "I ask myself," he said in a 1961 newspaper interview, "why I studied law. I don't know. I attribute it partly to those who said, 'He talks a lot, he ought to be a lawyer.' "[2] Given Fidel's lack of enthusiasm for formal scholarship, he chose well.

In Cuba the law was a field of study with low academic standards. A student with Fidel's ability to memorize could get by without much intellectual effort. Best of all, the study of law gave him time to use student politics to promote himself and make his mark as he had done with sports in high school. Fidel jumped into the boil of politics with reckless enthusiasm. It almost got him killed.

Violent politics was a long-standing tradition in Cuba. Despite failed revolutions, in the Cuba of 1945 the revolutionary spirit still smoldered, fueled by the same problems—poverty, social inequality, and political corruption—that had prompted earlier attempts at change. Always there were promises that change would come.

The president of Cuba, Ramón Grau San Martín, had been the candidate of new hope. He had come to power in 1944 on campaign promises of reform and good government, the new broom to sweep away the accumulated filth of Cuban politics. Unfortunately, the broom soon fell apart. Grau's regime lapsed into the same sad state of corruption, inefficiency, and disregard for the lower classes that had characterized those of his predecessors.

The University of Havana soon became the center of opposition to Grau, as it had been to earlier governments. It was not, however, a case of the white hats against the black hats. The university, too, was a corrupt institution, and much of the political activity there was conducted by groups that bore more resemblance to the Mafia or Los Angeles street gangs than to legitimate political reform groups. Because the groups battled one another as much as they opposed the government, the campus became a war zone. It was, in the words of Cuban journalist Carlos Franqui, a case of "gang warfare disguised as revolutionary politics." [3] University life was a dangerous undertaking, especially for those involved in politics. Many students, Fidel included, regularly carried guns for protection. The sounds of shootouts often echoed between the stately buildings of the university. Years later, Fidel recalled that his life had been more dangerous as a law student than as a revolutionary in the mountains of the Sierra Maestra.

The dominant student gangs were the Movimiento Socialista Revolucionaria (the Socialist Revolutionary Movement, or MSR) and the rival Unión Insurreccional Revolucionaria (Insurrectional Revolutionary Movement, or UIR). Apparently Fidel steered clear of the gangs for a time and focused on winning leadership in the more conventional student groups. That he was not successful suggests that his charisma and famous speaking ability had not yet matured.

One of Fidel's earliest attempts to lead students in opposition to the government occurred when he organized a protest against rising bus fares. Police attacked the demonstrators, and Fidel received a head wound which he used to great advantage. He went to a local hospital, got his head bandaged, then made the rounds of local newspapers and radio stations. He had a knack for getting noticed, and it paid off. In an effort to defuse the unrest over the bus fares, President Grau agreed to meet with several leaders of the protest. Fidel, looking the part of the wounded young scholar, went as a member of the delegation. At one point, he suggested to his companions that they throw Grau off the balcony of the presidential palace and proclaim the success of the student revolution.[4]

Fidel couldn't get elected to anything in the respectable student organizations. This failure pushed him toward the most powerful student gangs, the MSR and the UIR. It was the beginning of Fidel's gangster period, a time that earned him a reputation for violent activities. His enemies have charged that he killed at least two people, but no confirming evidence has ever surfaced. The American journalist Herbert Matthews addressed these charges in a 1969 Castro biography and reasoned, "If Fidel Castro had really killed anybody during his university years, convincing evidence would have been found by his Cuban enemies and the United States CIA."[5] On the other hand, if Fidel did not actually kill someone, it was not for lack of effort.

In December 1946, Fidel participated in an attack on Leonel Gómez, a prominent student leader and member of the UIR. The purpose of the attack was to gain favor with the leadership of the rival MSR. Standing on top of a hill, Fidel and two other attackers fired at Gomez as he drove his car on a street below. Fidel later related the incident to his friend and future brother-in-law, Rafael Díaz-Balart. ". . . [T]he three started to fire wildly and several persons walking below were wounded. But

Fidel's eyes gleamed. He was perfectly calm then. . . . He took aim and he shot."[6] Fidel believed that he had killed Gomez, but, though shot in the lungs, the UIR leader survived and named him as one of the attackers. Nothing came of the accusation. Ironically, despite the attack on one of its prominent members and for reasons which are not very clear, the UIR eventually took Fidel in as a member. It was not to be a satisfying relationship.

The UIR did not provide Fidel with opportunities for advancement. A rebellious loner, he did not fit into any organization requiring cooperation and obedience to an authority not his own. He needed a wider platform on which to maneuver and build a name for himself. Fidel's opportunity came in 1947 when a ragtag group of revolutionaries attempted to overthrow the government of Generalísimo Rafael Leónidas Trujillo in the neighboring Dominican Republic.

Trujillo had exercised dictatorial powers in the Dominican Republic since May of 1930, when he bullied his way into the presidency. He was the classic Latin America *caudillo* whose regime over the next thirty-one years would set record highs for corruption, brutality, and despicable behavior. Chief among those of his Dominican countrymen who sought to depose him was the patriot Juan Bosch. Trujillo was not liked in Cuba, and Bosch used Havana as a base of operation from which to organize and launch a revolutionary campaign. Bosch brought together an international collection of revolutionaries—some 1,200 of them uneasily cemented together by their hatred of Trujillo—from Santo Domingo, Cuba, Costa Rica, Venezuela, and Guatemala. Many of the Cubans were students. Several were Fidel's enemies from the gangs. They all agreed to observe a temporary truce for the duration of the Dominican campaign, and Fidel was given charge of a small unit of the enthusiastic, if inexperienced, volunteers. Enthusiasm, as it turned out, was no substitute for experience, careful planning, and good sense. The assault against Trujillo was doomed from the start because no one could keep a secret.

Fidel and the others trained at a remote spot called Cayo Confites, on the coast of Oriente Province. Little effort was made to maintain security, and by the time the three ships of the Cayo Confites expedition set sail for the Dominican Republic, much of Latin America—including Generalissimo Trujillo—knew of it. Trujillo used his influence with the United States government to place political pressure on Cuba to stop the invasion. President Grau ordered a halt to the expedition, and the ships turned back to Cuba, carrying their cargos of demoralized and thoroughly disgusted revolutionaries.

When the ships neared the Oriente coast of Cuba, Fidel jumped overboard, either to avoid capture by the Cuban military or to escape attack by his rivals—perhaps both. According to the legend that grew up around this incident, he swam over 8 miles (12.8 km) through shark-infested waters while holding a machine gun above his head. Fidel successfully avoided capture and made his way to the Castro estate in Birán. Though his first effort at becoming a revolutionary with international credentials was a failure, there would soon be other such opportunities.

In 1948, the United Nations sponsored a meeting of leaders of the Americas in Bogotá, Colombia, to create a cooperative regional group, the Organization of American States (OAS). Many leftists interpreted the proposal as yet another instance of the United States extending its imperialistic fingers into the internal affairs of Latin America. Fidel Castro was one of the organizers of an anti-imperialist congress in Bogotá aimed at countering the proposed OAS and especially the extension of "Yankee" influence.

The opposing groups met simultaneously in April of 1948. Fidel, representing the law school of the University of Havana, arrived in Bogotá in late March to begin the work of organizing popular protests. One of those he contacted for support was the Colombian opposition leader, Jorge Eliecer Gaitán, who agreed to assist the students.

On April 9, just minutes before a scheduled meeting with Castro and another student leader, Gaitán was shot to death in the street outside his office. Social unrest was so widespread in Bogotá that Gaitán's death sparked a bloody and destructive reaction in the city. This spontaneous demonstration against the government came to be called the *Bogotázo*. The violent uprising caused the destruction by fire of nearly one third of the city and the deaths of some 5,000 people. Fidel, never one to avoid action, was in the middle of the violent and frenzied events.

One eyewitness put Fidel at the scene "armed with a rifle" and part of a mob "drunk with the looting, burning and shooting." [7] In an interview years later, Fidel played down his participation.

On the ninth of April I joined a crowd marching on a police station. . . . I did what every student in Colombia did. I joined the people. As far as my real participation is concerned, I tried, insofar as it was possible, to avoid the fire-bombing and vandalism that caused that rebellion to fail. But my actions didn't amount to a drop in the bucket. . . . My conduct could not have been more disinterested or altruistic. . . . [8]

When the raging fires of the Bogotázo had cooled and the dead had been carried away, the Colombian government attempted to affix blame for the mass disturbance. Soon there were charges of a Communist conspiracy, to which the name of Fidel Castro was linked as a leader. Subsequent investigation revealed no evidence of Communist involvement. Fidel was no more than he seemed, a student agitator and enthusiastic anti-American troublemaker with no apparent links to the Communist party.

The Bogotá uprising, powered by the anger and frustration of the masses, failed to destroy the rightist government of Colombia. It was like an explosion with limited fuel and no specific direction. Fidel Castro, returning to Cuba in a cargo plane, came home having learned some important lessons about the nature of popular uprisings and how they can fail without organization and strong leadership. He would clearly remember the tumultuous times in Colombia and would apply those lessons to Cuba.

Returning to the relative peace of university life, Fidel, during the next few years, entered what was for him a reasonably quiet phase of his life. Given the record of his grades, he seems to have concentrated more on his studies. Also, he cooled his involvement in student gangsterism for more mainline political connections. And he played more baseball.

Fidel was such a hot prospect as a pitcher that he was scouted by several American major league baseball teams. Joe Cambria, scout for the old Washington Senators, wrote in his report to the home office, "Fidel Castro is a big, powerful young man. His fastball is not great, but passable. He uses good curve variety. He uses his head and can win that way for us, too." A Giants scout noted that Fidel was a "gentleman . . . a nice young man to deal with . . . stable."[9] The Giants were impressed enough to offer him a $5,000 contract to play in the United States.

Fidel turned down the career opportunity, saying he wanted to finish his law studies. Instead of playing baseball, he got married.

Fidel Castro Ruz married Mirta Díaz-Balart on October 10, 1948. Mirta was a student in the department of philosophy and letters at the University of Havana. Rafael Díaz-Balart, Fidel's friend and Mirta's brother, introduced the couple. Even the self-centered Fidel could fall in love. The physical attraction was strong. Fidel was no longer the rough-and-tumble gangster of his early student days. His height, patrician carriage, sharply sculpted Spanish profile, and piercing brown eyes—the air of danger and *machismo*—made him attractive to young women. Mirta was green-eyed and petite, a dark-haired beauty whose well-to do family connections both fascinated and repelled a young revolutionary.

It was a poor match, but given Fidel's personality and interests, was probably the best he was capable of making. He had neither the time nor the inclination for the traditional role of husband and father. Mirta's people were strongly opposed to the marriage. Her father, staunchly middle class, was mayor of the town of Banes in Oriente Province. Banes was a little America, a creation of United Fruit and other Yankee-owned interests. In her biography of Fidel, Georgia Anne Geyer showed the different worlds of the young couple with her description of Banes.

> Here, instead of the enveloping dark forests that Angel [Castro] cut away with so much sweat, were luxurious lawns and impressive tropical homes. Here American and Cuban employees of United Fruit played polo, swam in their pleasant swimming pools, and shopped in boutiques for American goods. . . . Here one found in Mirta's Banes a burgeoning and upward-striving middle class of Cubans who lived like Americans, prayed like Americans. . . . Banes had more ties to New York than Havana.[10]

Fidel appears to have had genuine feelings for Mirta, but part of his fascination with her must have been the opportunity to tweak the nose of the bourgeois society he despised by stealing away one of its beautiful daughters. Certainly Mirta's father knew of Fidel's reputation for gangsterism. Did he know that the man kneeling next to his daughter at the altar had a gun in his pocket—protection against possible attack by student gangs? Fidel joked about it afterward. Díaz-Balart must have wondered what kind of husband his daughter was getting.

The wedding was celebrated in the high style and wealthy display appropriate to the joining of two well-to-do families. Fidel could enjoy luxury, even though as a revolutionary he officially despised it. Nor did he appear to have any compunction about accepting large gifts of money from his father-in-law and from rich friends of the two families. As Fidel's relationship with his own father showed, he didn't need to like people to accept their money. It was a compromise of principle he would exhibit later when raising funds for the revolution.

On the very day the handsome young couple exchanged promises, the new president of Cuba, Carlos Prío Socarrás, took the oath of office. He promised the people of Cuba a new era of good government. Both relationships, which seemed destined for happiness, were soon beset by problems of incompatibility.

The newlyweds, financed by a generous gift of $10,000 from Mirta's father and, ironically, another $1,000 from the man Fidel would eventually oust from power, Fulgencio Batista—a friend of both families—honeymooned in the United States. This was the first of several trips to the States for Fidel, but the only one on which he could simply be a tourist. The Castros began their three-month stay in Miami, then traveled north by train to New York. They met Mirta's brother, Rafael, who lived with his wife in Manhattan, and took a furnished apartment in the same building. While in New York Fidel used part of his honeymoon money to buy a car—not just any car but a shiny white Lincoln-Continental, big and flashy like his ambition.

Fidel and Mirta returned to Havana by ferry from Key West, Florida, having enjoyed their time in the United States. Life at home was more difficult as the couple settled into harsher economic realities and built a life for themselves apart from the affluence of their families. Fidel was not a good breadwinner. Though he joined the law firm of Azpiazu, Castro, and Rosende, he had few clients, and these were usually too poor to pay very much. The couple lived in modest apartments and depended on the financial largess of the Díaz-Balart family.

Their only child, named Fidelito after his father, was born in September 1949. Sometimes there was not enough milk for the baby, and there were always debts—to the electric company, the butcher, the grocer.

As the first blush of enthusiasm for married life faded, the relationship between Mirta and Fidel began to deteriorate. Fidel did not have enough staying power for a marriage and family. His thoughts and energies were elsewhere. He was often not at home, especially as he became more involved as a member and then leader of Eduardo "Eddy" Chibás's Ortodoxos (Orthodox) party.

Chibás had created the Orthodox party to provide opposition to the government of Ramón Grau San Martin. Fidel actively fought the re-election of Grau. In January 1947 he signed a declaration in which students pledged to sacrifice their lives for the cause of freedom. "It is better to die on your feet," they proclaimed, "than to live on your knees."[11]

Grau lost the presidential election of 1948. It was his former secretary of the interior, Carlos Prío Socarrás, who was sworn in as president of Cuba on Fidel's wedding day. Prío promised clean government, but his regime was soon mired in the mud of scandal and political corruption. Faced with the same old story, Fidel and the other members of the Orthodox party turned their criticism from Grau to Prío. Fidel was not much of a force in the party until Eddy Chibás unknowingly promoted him.

In 1952, Chibás attempted to galvanize public opinion against the government, "to awaken the civic conscience of the Cuban people," he said before the event. He shot himself during a broadcast of his popular weekly radio show. Fidel, ever the opportunist, used the death of Chibás to advance himself. He took over the plans for the funeral in order to position himself in the public eye and benefit from the outpouring of sentiment from Chibás supporters.

Following the death of Chibás, Fidel felt sure enough of himself within the Orthodox party to run for the Cuban House of Representatives on the Orthodox ticket. The party did not officially support him because of his radical reputation. Angel Castro, however, did contribute financially to Fidel's campaign, probably seeing it as a move toward respectability by his son.

The Orthodox party leaders gave Fidel little chance of success, but like so many others, then and later, underestimated his cleverness and his ability to advance his cause by sheer determination and hard work. Fidel was relentless in his courting of voters. He used a new style of letter campaign, often seen today, in which a form letter is made to look as if it has been handwritten. Each of the 100,000 Orthodox party voters on Fidel's list received a card from Fidel asking for his vote. He also took every opportunity to talk to the voters, often speaking several times in one evening. He was on the road constantly and spent even less time at home with Mirta and Fidelito.

In his pursuit of public office, did Fidel really believe that the democratic process could bring needed change to Cuba? Only in part. At this stage in his political thinking, success through the ballot box was only a means to a revolutionary end. He later recalled,

> I was ... thinking of a preliminary political stage for preparing the movement and a second stage of seizing power in a revolutionary way.... I was thinking of using certain positions as a platform from which to launch a revolutionary program—initially in the form of legislative bills.... [12]

As Fidel pursued his campaign for public office, he gained a popular following among those who had once looked to Eddy Chibás for inspiration. His effectiveness as a speaker, his ability to capture the interest and imagination of an audience, grew immensely. In the early months of 1952, he attracted and held crowds with fiery attacks on the corrupt administration of Carlos Prío.

Had Fidel Castro succeeded in his bid to capture a seat in the House of Representatives, the future might well have turned out differently. But the election never happened. On March 10, 1952—two months before the scheduled election—former President Fulgencio Batista overthrew the government of Carlos Prío. The bloodless coup, staged with the backing of the army, was over in a matter of minutes. Prío fled the country.

Batista seized power, as many strong men had done before him throughout Latin America, in the name of good order, freedom, and democracy. He claimed it was a preemptive strike made necessary by Prío's intention to overthrow the election and seize the presidency. Few took that possibility seriously.

Fidel lost no time in attacking Batista and his supporters, accusing them of "a brutal snatching of power." In an emotional declaration and call to action issued three days after the coup, Fidel characterized the members of the new government as "destroyers of freedom, . . . adventurers thirsty for gold and power. . . ." He reminded the people of Cuba "that there is infinite happiness in fighting against oppression, in raising a strong hand and saying, I do not want to be a slave!" His declaration closed with the last lines of the Cuban national anthem, "To live in chains is to live sunk in shame and dishonor. To die for the fatherland is to live." [13]

Despite his rhetoric, Fidel was not planning to die for his country anytime soon. He knew he would be a target in the inevitable crackdown against critics of the new government. Soon after the coup was announced, he left his house and took refuge with his half-sister, Lydia. He escaped Batista's police by minutes and was on the run for the next sixteen months, always staying just a few steps ahead of the authorities. Of course, going home to his wife and family was out of the question, except for the occasional stolen moment. It was a stressful time for Mirta and Fidelito. Fidel's family life was a casualty of his political ambitions.

By the middle of 1953, working underground, Fidel had fashioned a modest following of dissidents. These were not the followers and hangers-on of his university days but were mostly men and women of the lower-middle or working classes. They were loyal to lesser leaders who were, in turn, loyal to Fidel. Most of Fidel's supporters were not even members of the Orthodox party. His allegiance to the party had waned since the coup, and he criticized its leadership for its lack of resistance to the Batista regime. Certainly he had himself in mind when he wrote in 1953 that the "vacuum of leadership" would be filled "by tougher men from the ranks." This new breed of leader would seize the revolutionary moment, "take up the battle standard," and "save Cuba." [14]

Fidel was prepared to back up his bold words with bold actions. He would strike directly at Batista's base of power, the army. He devised a plan to capture two military barracks in Oriente Province. Removed from the concentration of military power in Havana, such attacks, Fidel reasoned, stood a chance of succeeding. Taking the Moncada barracks in Santiago and another in nearby Bayamo could spark a popular uprising in volatile Oriente Province, with its long history of revolutionary fervor. The uprising might then spread to the rest of the country. Even if it did not, the capture of a substantial amount of arms and ammunition would both equip Fidel's followers for future resistance and score an important propaganda victory for the revolution.

It was a desperate scheme based more on the idea of heroic action than on carefully reasoned principles. "The Hymn of the 26 July" composed by Augustín Díaz Cartaya shortly before the attack proclaimed to the world,

> ... we are soldiers
> Going to free the country
>
> Cleansing with fire
> Which will destroy this infernal plague

Of bad governments
And insatiable tyrants
Who have plunged Cuba into evil.[15]

Fidel chose July 26, 1953, as the day for his two-pronged attack for both symbolic and practical reasons. It was the anniversary of the death of José Martí, the great Cuban patriot and revolutionary hero. Since Fidel saw himself as the Martí of a new era, it would be an auspicious day for the revolution. More practically, July 26 came during the traditional carnival celebration in Santiago. Carnival always meant revelry, dancing, carousing, and drinking on a grand scale. According to Fidel's reasoning, soldiers suffering from lack of sleep and massive hangovers would be ill prepared to repel an attack during the early morning hours. It was the weakest point of the plan.

Fidel's experience with the unsuccessful Cayo Confites expedition and the 1948 uprising in Bogotá had driven home the necessity for careful organization and secrecy. At Moncada he counted heavily on the element of surprise and the high morale of his recruits. It wasn't very much to count on. Of the 160 men and two women who assembled for the attack, few had much military experience, and none had trained together as a coordinated unit. They were a collection of strangers. Their armaments consisted of a pathetic collection of a few military-issue rifles, one old machine gun, an assortment of hunting rifles—many of small caliber—and a grab bag of handguns.

The rebels came mostly from Havana, arriving by car or public transportation. They met at a farmhouse to learn the details of the attack. Fidel was so concerned with security that only six people knew of the plan. Most of the rest had no idea that they would soon be risking their lives for the cause. Even Fidel's brother Raúl was kept in the dark and joined the group late. He may have been considered a security risk because of his communist affiliation. Fidel took no chances.

Donning purchased and homemade military uniforms in the early morning hours of July 26, the rebels split into two groups. A group of 134 would attack the Moncada barracks in Santiago; 26 would hit the smaller one at Bayamo. Early in the morning, twenty-six cars carrying the main strike group left the rendezvous for Santiago. Tension and expectation ran high as the tiny army moved through the city streets of Santiago toward Moncada.

The plan called for Fidel and the largest body of fighters to attack the barracks. Ten men under Raúl would supply covering fire from a nearby roof. The others, including the women and Fidel's second-in-command, Abel Santamaría, would occupy the nearby civil hospital to set up diverting fire and prepare for treating the wounded.

Raúl and Abel Santamaría were able to fulfill their assignments with no hitches. For Fidel's group, the plan fell apart almost immediately. The forces assigned to back up his main thrust got lost in the unfamiliar streets of the city. They were not on hand for the decisive first moments of the raid on which everything hinged. The rebels in the first car, among the sixty or so that found the main gate, disarmed the sentries and entered the barracks. Fidel, in the second car, met three heavily armed soldiers. One escaped to sound the alarm. The element of surprise was lost, and most of the fighting took place outside the barracks, rather than inside as planned. The army's superior fire power soon had the rebels pinned down. Hope for success quickly evaporated.

Fidel gave the order for retreat. Those who were not trapped ran for their lives. Raúl's squad members escaped by stripping away their outer uniforms and blending into the movement of civilians on the streets. Those at the hospital were unaware of the retreat. Realizing eventually that the plan had fallen apart, they hid themselves as patients in the hospital. The attack had disintegrated in less than sixty minutes. Survivors led by Fidel drove back to the farmhouse headquarters.

If Moncada had been a failure, the attack at Bayamo was a disaster. Once again, the advantage of surprise was lost. Fighting lasted for only fifteen minutes before the order to retreat was given.

At Bayamo, most of the rebels were killed or quickly captured. Fidel's initial losses at Moncada included two dead and many wounded. The government casualties also consisted of a large number of wounded and about eighteen enlisted men and officers killed.

Fidel and eighteen of his men gathered new weapons at the farmhouse and headed for the mountains of the Sierra Maestra. Within a few hours, government troops began to comb the countryside, picking up exhausted and demoralized rebels. They arrested Raúl as he headed away from Santiago on foot across country.

Fidel and his small band moved toward the high country of the Sierra. Occasionally, peasants provided some food and directions. Fidel could hear and see government patrols nearby. Exhausted, the survivors stopped for sleep without posting guard. It was a serious mistake, Fidel later admitted.

> That night we found a thatched-roof hut. . . . Seeking shelter from the fog, the mist, and the cold, we decided to stay there until dawn. What happened was that precisely at dawn—before we woke up—a patrol

came into the hut, and we woke up with their rifles against our chests. The most disagreeable sensation there can be is to be awakened by the enemy like that.[16]

Fidel was lucky. He might have been killed any number of times had it not been for the sympathetic intervention of the lieutenant in charge of the patrol. He kept his soldiers in check and disobeyed orders to take the rebels to the local military garrison, almost certainly a final resting place. Most of the other rebels did not share Fidel's good fortune.

It is likely that Moncada and Bayamo would soon have been forgotten by the Cuban public, passed off as just another episode of ineffectual violence perpetrated by yet another gang of dissidents. But the government behaved stupidly. It dealt with many of the surviving prisoners with such vengeful brutality that it aroused public opinion in favor of the rebels. Moncada became a *cause célèbre*, the stuff of which legends are made.

Soldiers murdered most of the rebels captured on July 26 and in the days following. Many of them were beaten with rifle butts or tortured in various other ways before being shot. Some were dragged to death behind jeeps. In prison, a soldier opened a bloody hand to show rebel fighter Haydée Santamaría the eye of her brother, Abel, and threatened to get the other if she did not tell everything. According to the legend that grew up around Moncada, her reply was, "If he did not tell you under torture, far less will I tell you." Of the 162 rebels participating in the attack on Moncada and Bayamo, 68 were killed. The government brought 32 of the survivors, including Fidel, to trial. The rest escaped.

People found out about the savagery of the government's actions through gossip and later newspaper accounts, despite attempts at censorship. Fidel

Castro in failure made the kind of mark on the Cuban public that he had hoped to achieve with successes. The fighters and martyrs of the 26 July Movement, as it came to be called, became the focus for a growing resistance to the Batista government.

CHAPTER THREE

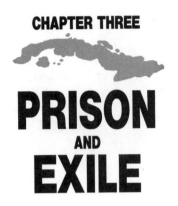

PRISON
AND
EXILE

The July assault on the army barracks at Santiago was a waste from the military point of view. In terms of enhancing Fidel Castro's credentials as a revolutionary, it was a roaring success. Moncada displayed Fidel's capability, undeveloped as it may have been, to plan and carry out a military operation, to function under fire, and most important to the future, to inspire men and women to follow him at the risk of their lives. Moncada and the trials resulting from it also provided Fidel with a stage from which to touch and move people with his ideas. Fidel had a talent for sizing up and seizing the moment. The Moncada trials presented Fidel with his first big opportunity. He used it brilliantly.

The Batista government brought Fidel and his companions to trial on September 21, 1953—almost two months after Moncada. Word of the government's brutal treatment of the captured rebels had leaked out to touch a nerve among those Cubans who were politically aware. There was an interested audience, both in Santiago and among those who would read the newspaper accounts of journalists attending the trial. Fidel had his stage, and the government played right into his hands.

First, guards brought him into the court of Santiago's Palace of Justice in handcuffs. Eloquently and dramatically, he appealed to the judges. The handcuffs were removed. Next, he won the right to represent himself in the court proceedings and donned the robes of the trial lawyer, giving an air of weight and legitimacy to his revolutionary language. The government soon realized what was happening and decided to try Fidel apart from his comrades and in secret, away from the spotlight of public opinion.

Fidel's trial took place on October 16, not at the grand Palace of Justice, but in the tiny nurse's lounge of the very same hospital where his comrades had attempted to hide from government soldiers. Still acting in his own defense, he appeared before three judges, two public prosecutors, and six journalists (who, by some accounts, were not allowed to take notes).

Not all of the pertinent facts of this episode in Fidel's career are clear. Much has become legend. Some say Fidel spoke for five hours on behalf of himself and the revolution. This, if we can judge from later and longer performances, was certainly within his abilities. The speech, incubated, amended, and expanded by Fidel in prison, eventually came to the outside world as a pamphlet titled "History Will Absolve Me."

Appearing before his judges after twenty-six days of solitary confinement, Fidel spoke "with words made of the blood of his own heart." He lashed out at his enemies. Fulgencio Batista was a "vicious, arrogant tyrant." His government was a collection of "the most inhuman gang of assassins it is possible to imagine." They were "political racketeers, the scum of . . . public life." He ridiculed the government's heavy-handed efforts to silence him. His captors had claimed at various times that he was either too ill to appear or had escaped. Of his trial in the lounge of a public hospital, he noted slyly that "it is unwise to administer justice from a hospital room, surrounded by sentinels with fixed bayonets; the citizens might suppose that our justice is sick—and that it is captive." [1] This was just the opening shot.

Fidel's most well known speech is very long, running over a hundred pages in some editions. Besides reviling the Batista government for its overthrow of Cuban democracy, Fidel told the story of Moncada and Bayamo, characterizing it as a true revolutionary movement created by and for the people. For effect, he emphasized, though apparently did not exaggerate, the merciless treatment many of his comrades had suffered at the hands of the army after the failed attacks.

> The Moncada Barracks were turned into a workshop of torture and death. Some abject individuals turned their uniforms into butcher's aprons. The walls were spattered with blood. The bullets embedded in the walls were encrusted with singed bits of skin, brains and human hair, the grisly reminders of rifle shots full in the face. The grass around the barracks was dark and sticky with human blood. [2]

Most important to Fidel's career, "History Will Absolve Me" set out the revolutionary principles that became the political backbone of the 26 July Movement. Fidel never stopped paying allegiance to these principles—though later critics would claim he certainly departed from them. Fidel announced to the assembled judges that his five "Revolutionary Laws" had been waiting in the wings at Moncada, ready to be proclaimed to the world.

The First Revolutionary Law was Fidel's tribute to democracy. It "returned power to the people and proclaimed the Constitution of 1940 the supreme law of the state, until such time as the people should decide to modify or exchange it."[3] The second law aimed to distribute land to landless farmers, making the state responsible for reimbursing the former owners. Revolutionary Laws Three and Four created profit sharing for both industrial and agricultural workers. The fifth law promised that everything that previous governments and individuals had stolen from the people would be, one way or another, returned to the people.

Once the basic laws had been put into effect, Fidel claimed, they would be followed by a flurry of needed social and economic changes: land reform, development of education, lower utility rates, better tax collection for the wealthy, state-sponsored employment, improved health care, and more modern living conditions. The beneficiary of these changes, Fidel announced, was to be "The People." The people included the vast army of unemployed, farmers without any hope of owning land, industrial workers living in impoverished conditions, small business people, and the young professionals who believed in democracy and social justice. Fidel called them "the vast unredeemed masses, to whom all make promises . . . the people who yearn for a better, more dignified and more just nation."[4] The ideas that Fidel presented in his speech were broad enough to have a wide appeal among most Cubans but vague enough not to frighten off those who may have been leery of stronger, more radical language. Fidel was smart about working for a broad base of support, especially when he was politically weak.

Fidel closed his long speech by establishing Moncada and July 26, 1953, as a link in the chain constituting humanity's acts of rebellion against tyranny. He spoke of China, India, ancient Greece and Rome. He paraphrased thinkers from Thomas Aquinas to Thomas Paine. He celebrated the American and French Revolutions. And he quoted the famous passage of the American Declaration of Independence which begins, "We hold these truths to be self-evident, that all Men are created equal, that they are endowed by their Creator with certain unalienable Rights, that among these are Life, Liberty and the Pursuit of Happiness. . . ." Finally, Fidel ended his defense with the words which have become famous far beyond the borders of Cuba.

> I know that imprisonment will be as hard for me as it has ever been for anyone, filled with cowardly threats and wicked torture. But I do not fear prison, as I do not fear the fury of the miserable tyrant who took the lives of seventy of my comrades.
> Condemn me. It does not matter. History will absolve me.[5]

Fidel's last line, "History will absolve me," came from an early speech of Adolf Hitler, whose style he had practiced and emulated as a schoolboy at Belén. The future Fuhrer of Germany made the same claim in 1924 when, like Fidel, he spoke at his own trial following a failed attempt to overthrow the government.

The court did condemn Fidel—to fifteen years in prison on the Isle of Pines. The other leaders, Raúl Castro and Pedro Miret, received thirteen years, and all the other men from three to ten years. The women, Melba Hernández and Haydée Santamaría, were not imprisoned. Owing to the unusual character of Cuban politics and a serious mistake in judgment by President Fulgencio Batista, the prisoners would all be released within two years.

The government transported Fidel and the other

Moncada prisoners to the Presidio, a huge prison on the Isle of Pines, 60 miles (96.5 km) south of the mainland. What the government viewed as the incarceration of dangerous rebels, Fidel saw as an opportunity—to read, to think, to educate loyal followers, and to plan a revolution.

The Presidio was no country club, but after some initially rough treatment, Fidel, as a political prisoner, achieved a kind of gentlemanly status that allowed him considerable freedom. He read incessantly and had access to a wide range of books, including works by Karl Marx. Politically he went on the offensive, as much as being in jail would allow. Letters moved freely in and out of prison. Right under the government's nose, Fidel used this freedom to maintain ties with other opposition groups.

Cuba's old-line Communists had decided on a policy of limited cooperation with Batista. They criticized and belittled the Moncada attack and branded Fidel as an adventurer. He would not forget. He chose to work with other groups, even his competitors for political influence. Eventually he would reject them, even eliminate them. For now he could use them against Batista. As he wrote to the Moncada women, Haydée and Melba, his advice was to:

> . . . show much guile and smiles to everybody. Follow the same course which we followed in the trial: defend your points of view without wounding others. We will have time later on to trample underfoot all the cockroaches. . . . Accept all sorts of help, but, remember, trust in no one.[6]

While others worked on his behalf against the Batista government on the outside, Fidel worked to strengthen the revolutionary movement inside the walls of prison. He organized a school for the development of revolutionary thinking and gave it the name of his comrade murdered at Moncada. The Abel Santamaría Ideological Academy became Fidel's tool for building solidarity and unity of purpose among the Moncada survivors.

Though mostly in solitary confinement, there were times each day when he was allowed contact with the others. On these occasions he lectured on philosophy and world history. Others in the group taught arithmetic, geography, English, and other school subjects. Fidel molded a highly disciplined and orderly group.

Ironically, prison authorities regarded the *Fidelistas*, who were working so diligently to overthrow the entire system, as model prisoners. They were not, however, always "good." On one occasion when President Batista visited the Isle of Pines to dedicate a power plant, he received a revolutionary serenade. Fidel recalled the incident in a conversation with Frei Betto.

> The power plant was very near the pavilion where we were, and one comrade, Juan Almeida, looked out a window and saw Batista when he went into the plant. We waited until he came out, and then we sang the "July 26th Anthem."
>
> At first, Batista thought it was all part of the welcoming ceremony or that it was perhaps a chorus singing his praises. At first he was happy, and he told the others ... to be quiet. Then he grew silent and began to get irritated when the words of our anthem spoke of the "insatiable tyrants who have plunged Cuba into evil." [7]

During the long months in his cell, Fidel paced the 12-by-12-foot (3.65-by-3.65-meter) floor, rocked in his rocking chair, and spent a great amount of time reconstructing and embellishing his Moncada trial defense. Writing between the lines of letters to his comrades, he used lime juice as invisible ink to smuggle out the "History Will Absolve Me" text piece by piece. His correspondents carefully ironed the letters to reveal the hidden writing. Eventually the entire speech was reassembled, and thousands of copies were printed and distributed quietly throughout the countryside.

Fidel kept some secrets better than others. His wife, Mirta, had supported him faithfully before and since his imprisonment. Fidel was not so faithful and for some years had a mistress, Naty Revuelta, a beautiful married woman he met at an Orthodox party meeting in 1952. Their affair was like a much-used movie plot: the well-to-do, upper-bourgeois woman falls for the seedy-looking but exciting and slightly dangerous radical. While Fidel has had several such relationships over the years, he has never been known as much of a "ladies' man" or "womanizer." A twenty-four-hour-a-day revolutionary, he probably never had the time.

Naty's glamour and vivacity must have offered a sharp contrast to Fidel's home scene: the responsibilities of a wife and baby, a shabby apartment, and piles of unpaid bills. He kept the secret of his double life from Mirta until the day in prison he made the mistake of writing to them both. When Mirta received the letter intended for Naty, Fidel's stock immediately dropped. Perhaps the switch was no mistake.

From that time their marriage, already over-stressed by Fidel's vagabond life and his seeming inability to accept the role of husband and father, deteriorated quickly. Their estrangement grew when Fidel learned, much to his embarrassment, that Mirta had been on the Batista government's payroll. Mirta's brother, Raphael Díaz-Balart, had quietly arranged a small pension—less than $100 a month—for her support. This kind of free ride for one's relatives—known in Spanish as a *botella*—was not an uncommon practice in a government riddled with corruption.

For Fidel, who always tried to present his revolutionary program in the strongest moral light, Mirta's acceptance of the government's money—never mind how badly she needed it—was unforgivable. Soon after this family scandal became public, Mirta filed for a divorce. Losing his son, Fidelito, to the influence of Mirta's family, those "miserable Judases,"[8] as he called them, was probably the hardest part of the dissolution of Fidel's marriage. On the other hand, it gave him more time for his most absorbing interest, pushing himself forward politically.

In prison Fidel achieved much of the recognition that had eluded him on the outside. Because of the publicity surrounding Moncada, he became a symbol of resistance to the illegal Batista government. In the words of historian Hugh Thomas, he was "the spirit of liberty incarcerated and of Martí reincarnated." Even so, Fidel was not a household word in Cuba. Those who cared about him and what he stood for constituted a limited audience. His impact as an opposition leader was not yet great.

Since the coup in July Batista had done much to consolidate his position and gain acceptance by the Cuban people. He had eliminated much of the effective political opposition; his enemies were in prison or in exile. The Cuban economy appeared stable, and the outlook for a large and profitable sugar harvest was rosy. Internationally, Batista had won approval of American president Dwight D. Eisenhower as the U.S.'s strongman of choice to maintain peace and stability. In the Cold War atmosphere of competing ideologies, America valued governments whose policies protected her economic interests and resisted Communism. The Batista government appeared to do both.

Despite attacks by the opposition, Batista's popularity rose among many Cubans. They saw, or thought they saw, improvements: less turmoil and gangsterism in political life; fewer cases of corruption in public office; and calmer labor relations, evidenced by fewer strikes. Batista began to feel more secure in his stolen presidency. Having power, he sought to win legitimacy. Even before Fidel had been imprisoned, Batista had announced a general election for November 1, 1954. Cleverly, he declined to say whether or not he would be a candidate for president.

When the election came, Batista made sure he was the only candidate. He won. Technically he was now the lawfully elected president of Cuba, though the opposition, including Fidel from prison, criticized the entire election proceedings as illegal and farcical. Batista went from strength to strength. U.S. vice-president Richard M. Nixon put America's stamp of approval on Batista with a visit in February 1955. Nixon was followed by Allen Dulles, director of the Central Intelligence Agency (CIA), who came to inspect and approve Cuba's anti-Communist program.

Feeling very much in charge and facing no effective opposition, Batista believed he could afford to be generous. He followed the Cuban tradition of celebrating presidential electoral victories by declaring a general amnesty for political prisoners. The amnesty included the Moncada rebels. The government released Fidel and the others from prison on May 15, 1955. Batista's burst of generosity would turn out to be a terrible mistake in judgment. It would not be the last time he underestimated Fidel Castro.

Fidel's release, coming as it did when Batista was strong and popular, caused hardly a ripple on the pond of Cuban political life. The opposition, such as it was, existed in a state of uncertainty. Was it better to fight Batista or compromise with him and work for political reform? Fresh out of prison, Fidel faced his own uncertainty about where he fit in the current political scene. Some of his support from the time of Moncada had melted away. He no longer had much influence among students at the University of Havana. New leaders with different ideas had risen in his absence.

Despite his recent release from prison, Fidel refused to accept the Batista government and renewed his vocal criticisms immediately. Though revolution was still his goal, it soon became clear that Havana was no place to prepare it. Batista's secret police intended to kill him and make it look as if he had been the victim of a rival group. Fidel gathered together the 26 July Movement (the Moncada group with some additions), and made plans to leave Cuba for Mexico to build a revolution. In a letter to prominent political leaders dated on the day of his departure, July 7, 1955, he announced:

> I am leaving Cuba because all doors of peaceful struggle have been closed to me. Six weeks after being released from prison I am convinced more than ever of the dictatorship's intention to remain in power . . . , ruling as now by the use of terror and crime. . . . As a follower of Martí, I believe the hour has come to take rights and not to beg for them, to fight instead of pleading for them.
>
> I will reside somewhere in the Caribbean.
>
> From trips such as this, one does not return, or else one returns with the tyranny beheaded at one's feet.[9]

Mexico in the summer of 1955 was hot and the hotbed of political conspiracy in Latin America. Because of its liberal political environment, it seemed to Fidel to be the one place where an expedition could be readied for an invasion of Cuba—if the conspirators exercised caution. There was danger. The tentacles of the Cuban secret police extended throughout the Caribbean. Fidel understood the need for secrecy.

Fidel made contact with other exiles from Batista's Cuba who were willing to make a revolution in the name of the 26 July Movement and Fidel Castro. For security reasons he created small, separate revolutionary units, or cells, and housed them in six rented houses scattered around Mexico City. The Fidelistas began training for the invasion by jogging the wide avenues of the city and rowing on the lake of the city park. Fidel continued the war of words with the *Manifesto Number 1 to the People of Cuba* which was smuggled to Cuba inside a hollowed-out book. The *Manifesto* set forth a fifteen-point program, an elaboration of the ideas for reform which had appeared in the earlier "History Will Absolve Me" speech. It also issued an open call for revolution. "The bridges have been burned," wrote Fidel. "Either we conquer the fatherland at any price so that we can live with dignity and honor, or we shall remain without one." [10]

But these were words, not bullets, and the Cuban government seemed impervious to words. Batista had been in power for four years. Though the democratic opposition at home had attempted to unite, nothing happened to lever Batista out of power. There were incidents: occasional student riots in Havana and Santiago, several protests of sugar workers, some bombings by members of the 26 July Movement.

Batista's secret police met protest and violence with hard reaction: arrests, beatings, torture, and killings. All opposition was neutralized. As historian Hugh Thomas observed, "The few bombs exploding in back streets and Castro's activity in Mexico seemed like freak hailstorms, disagreeable, inexplicable but unimportant and soon forgotten." [11] Fidel knew that he could not challenge the Batista government by long distance. He had to carry the fight home. For that he needed money.

There was money to be had in the north. Following in the steps of his hero Martí, who organized the 1895 revolution from the United States, Fidel met with Cuban expatriates in Tampa, Miami, and New York to raise money for his plan of national liberation. "We are doing with the émigrés," he announced in a 1955 New York speech, "the things our Apostle Martí taught us in a similar situation."

From this same platform he also proclaimed that the revolution would begin in the following year. "I can inform you with complete reliability that in 1956 we will be free or we will be martyrs. This struggle . . . will end with the last day of the dictatorship or our death." [12] Fidel raised money among the Cuban exiles in Mexico and the United States, exiles from Venezuela, and others sympathetic to left-wing causes. Ex-President Prío was his largest single contributor, committing $100,000 to the overthrow of Batista in hopes of reestablishing himself at the head of the Cuban government. While Fidel was happy to take Prío's money, he had no intention of serving Prío's ambition.

Fidel returned to Mexico to continue building his expedition. Training took place under the guiding hand of Albert Bayo, a Spanish-Cuban living in Mexico and a soldier with considerable military experience in Spain and North Africa. Bayo began weapons training at a firing range in Mexico City; then Fidel moved the operation to a more secluded setting, a ranch called Santa Rosa twenty miles (32 km) outside the city. They trained with a variety of arms and explosives and learned the techniques of night fighting. Bayo was a hard taskmaster and pushed the men to the limit in their new roles as guerrilla fighters.

In July 1955, Fidel met Ernesto "Che" Guevara, destined to become a legend in the revolutionary politics of Latin America. Guevara was twenty-six years old. A doctor by training, he was a revolutionary by temper of mind and heart, and had committed himself to Marxist ideals of social justice. Che had recently lived in Guatemala until the leftist government there had been overthrown by a partnership between the military and the American CIA. He had been searching for a leader and cause. In Fidel he found both.

At their first meeting, they talked through the night. They had much in common, including a great hostility toward the United States and its policies in Latin America. The two young men fit together— Che, the man of ideas, complementing the character of Fidel Castro, the man of action. Very soon Che Guevara became one of the four most important satellite figures revolving around Fidel in the early days of the revolution. The others were Frank País, head of the 26 July Movement (now just called M-26-7) action groups back in Cuba, and in Mexico Raúl Castro and Albert Bayo. Che Guevara joined the expedition as its doctor and soon began training as another of its guerrilla fighters.

As the military training continued in Mexico in 1955, Fidel stepped up the propaganda campaign in Cuba. Surprisingly, he had been receiving press coverage in Havana ever since his self-exile. Batista had lifted most of the censorship that had been imposed in the coup of 1952. As a result, the popular magazine *Bohemia* carried many of Fidel's letters and pronouncements from Mexico.

On April 1, 1956, *Bohemia* published an article

in which Fidel announced his formal break with the Orthodox party. He accused its leaders of doing nothing to oppose Batista and offering no more than "crocodile tears" to the memory of party founder Eduardo Chibás. Now, he wrote, his own 26 July Movement would be the true voice of the Cuban people, "the revolutionary organization of the humble, for the humble, and by the humble." [13]

Fidel was laying the groundwork for his return by elbowing out some of the competition and identifying himself and his group as the vanguard of the coming revolution. Yet, while the Batista government seemed to be taking Fidel a bit more seriously—in February a Havana court ordered his arrest—he was still just one of the pack in a field of competitors aiming to overthrow Fulgencio Batista.

The Cuban secret police monitored the activities of Fidel Castro as well as others, both at home and abroad, who posed any kind of threat to the current government. Because Fidel had publicly announced his intention to be in Cuba at the head of an army in 1956, Batista put pressure on the Mexican government to curtail this challenge to his power, however remote its chance of success might be.

The Mexican police responded by arresting Castro, Guevara, Bayo, and twenty-one others on June 22. They were singled out for preparing an attack on a neighboring sovereign state, a charge which could have caused jails to overflow if it had been used against all those conspiring against foreign governments in the Mexico of the 1950s. The Cuban secret police tried unsuccessfully to concoct evidence connecting Fidel to the activities of Communists in Mexico. They confused the facts enough to keep the Cuban rebels in prison for over a month.

The Mexican courts released Fidel and his followers on July 24. They immediately resumed their training, this time in greater secrecy. Still, Batista knew what Fidel was up to in Mexico but chose not to take more active and violent steps to eliminate the threat. Feeling secure at home, he underestimated Fidel's ability to make trouble from Mexico. It was another mistake in judgment, and it would cost Batista everything.

In the closing months of 1956, two family matters of differing emotional weight intruded on Fidel's preparations to "liberate the fatherland," as he called it. When it came time to land his forces on the coast of Oriente Province, he did not want his son, Fidelito, in Cuba, perhaps to become a hostage of the Batista government. He called Mirta and asked that the boy be allowed to visit him in Mexico for two weeks. She agreed only when she wrung from him a promise to return the boy after that time. Fidel made the promise. He had no intention of keeping it.

Fidelito arrived in Mexico on September 17. Fidel placed him with the family of a supporter, Alfonso Gutiérrez. His intention was to give the boy a new identity and a new life apart from his mother and the despised Díaz-Balart family. Fidel explained himself in a letter written on the day he left Mexico.

> I am making this decision because I do not want, in my absence, to see my son Fidelito in the hands of those who have been my most ferocious enemies and detractors, those who . . . attacked my home and sacrificed it to the interest of a bloody tyranny that they continue to serve. Because my wife has demonstrated herself to be incapable of breaking away from the influence of her family, my son could be educated with the detestable ideas that I now fight.[14]

The arrangement did not last. After Fidel's departure for Cuba, agents of the Cuban and Mexican governments snatched the boy and returned him to his mother. The second family matter was the death of Angel Castro in October. Fidel had never been close to his father. He shoved the telegram announcing the old man's death into his pocket and was, by most accounts, unaffected by the news.

In the last months of 1956, Fidel made final preparations to fulfill his promise of carrying the revolution to the fatherland. With some of the money advanced by Prió, the rebels purchased a boat to carry them across the Gulf of Mexico to Cuba. She was the *Granma*, a poorly maintained 38-foot (11.6-m) wooden yacht with two undersized engines.

The *Granma* was too small and too underpowered to carry eighty-five people over hundreds of miles of potentially rough sea. If Fidel understood this, he seemed not to care. As was often the case, his optimism and his bent for action pushed him on, outdistancing his common sense. But Fidel was a risk-taker. And he was lucky. He believed that the *Granma*, despite her inadequacies, would suffice.

Back in Cuba, Frank País, at the head of the M-26-7 action groups, began a campaign of sabotage and terrorism to pave the way for Fidel's arrival. In one incident, a group of university students belonging to the Directorio Revolucionario attacked police and military officers and their wives as they left a Havana nightclub. Among those killed was Batista's chief of military intelligence. The reprisals were swift and bloody.

País's orders were to provoke a general uprising in Santiago at the end of November to coordinate with Fidel's imminent landing on the coast of Oriente Province. Oriente, home to so much earlier revolutionary activity, would become Fidel's fuse to ignite an explosion of anti-Batista sentiment across Cuba.

In Mexico the rebels made their way in ones and twos to the sleepy port of Tuxpan on the Gulf coast, where the *Granma* awaited them. In the early-morning hours of November 25, the overloaded little boat, carrying Fidel and eighty-five of his followers, chugged its way into the Gulf of Mexico to keep Fidel's promise: *Revolucion o Muerta!* (Revolution or Death!)

CHAPTER FOUR

THE
REVOLUTION COMES HOME

Fidel's plan to carry the revolution home to Cuba was laced with risks. First, he had to get there in an overloaded and underpowered boat. Second, once in Cuban waters, he had to avoid detection by Batista's naval and air patrols. Third, he had to land at a specified place to make contact with his support group. Last, he had to coordinate his landing with Frank País' diversionary attack on Santiago. There were so many things to go wrong, and most of them did.

The revolution might easily have ended on the floor of the Gulf of Mexico. The *Granma* was a pleasure boat, not a troop carrier. Tiny engines strained to push the overloaded yacht through waves that threatened to swamp her. The eighty-six men aboard barely had room to sit down. Most of them were seasick in the rough waters and spent considerable time hanging their heads over the side of the boat, probably wishing they were back in Mexico. Fidel was not sick and, despite the conditions, full of talk as usual.

Fidel allotted five days for the voyage. The landing was timed to coordinate with the M-26-7 attack on Santiago. Frank País had traveled to Mexico months earlier to discuss the plan with Fidel. If possible, he would take control of the city. At least he would create a diversion to cover Fidel's landing. País argued against the plan, believing it too risky with the forces available. As usual, Fidel had his way.

On November 30, when the rebels should have landed, the *Granma* was still far from the Cuban coast. Helplessly they heard a radio broadcast reporting the attack on Santiago. Led by Frank País, 300 men wearing the arm bands of M-26-7 assaulted government buildings in the city. Many were killed in the wasted effort. The army was firmly in control of the city, and the *Granma* was still at sea. Their problems multiplied.

Fidel's expedition finally reached the Oriente coast on December 2, but not at the planned landing site. The *Granma* ran aground in the shallows of Los Cayuelos, several hundred yards from shore and many miles from where it should have been. A coast guard cutter spotted the boat and notified Batista's forces ashore. Abandoning valuable equipment, the rebels quickly left the half-sunken *Granma* and waded ashore through a swamp. It took three hours of hellish labor for the exhausted men to reach firm land. Their labors were just beginning.

Within an hour of coming ashore, they were under fire from a navy gunboat and the Cuban air force. With everyone running for cover, one group of rebels became separated from the main body. The rush of action confused the orderly progression of the revolution. This would happen many times in the next several weeks.

On Monday, December 3, the hungry rebels met

some peasant farmers who shared food. This was the beginning of the all-important support Fidel received from the local people of Oriente. The movement could not have survived without it. On the same day, the lost group reestablished contact. The combined force then moved eastward through sugarcane fields toward the mountains of the Sierra Maestra. Soldiers and airplanes combed the area to find them. The inexperienced rebel fighters were careless in covering their movements. Breaking off pieces of sugarcane to suck for energy, they left a trail of refuse for the soldiers of the Rural Guard to follow.

The revolution nearly came to an abrupt end on Wednesday, December 5. The exhausted rebels made camp at Alegría del Pío. The army surprised them late in the afternoon. It was, Fidel said later, the "worst moment" in his life. The cane fields around them erupted in a storm of automatic weapons fire and blasts from the bombs of attacking aircraft.

Once again the rebels scattered, taking cover where they could. A bullet caught Che Guevara in the shoulder. After several hours of fighting, some of the outgunned Fidelistas surrendered to the Rural Guardsmen, only to be shot soon after. Twenty-four revolutionaries died at Alegría del Pío.

Fidel and two of his men escaped but became separated from the others in the confusion of battle. For the next several days they hid out in nearby cane fields by burying themselves in piles of *paja*, cane debris, and lying as still as death. They heard planes making strafing runs over burning fields of cane. They listened tensely to the voices of soldiers passing nearby. Once again, Fidel's luck held.

It became quiet, but the three stayed put—a difficult exercise for the always active Commandante. Without food and water, they sucked the juice of sugarcane. Fidel slept with the barrel of a rifle at his throat. He vowed not to be taken alive. The three hid like rats in the cane fields for five days and nights.

Unable to be quiet for long periods, Fidel talked to himself and the others in hoarse whispers for hours at a stretch. He made plans for the future as if there would be one, spoke of revolutionary principles, and expressed the self-confidence and faith that burned so strongly in him. "We are winning," he told the others as they huddled miserably under the *paja*. "Victory will be ours."[1] His comrades could be forgiven for thinking him *loco*, crazy.

On December 11, the three left the fields to continue east. For all they knew, the rebel army consisted of its commander-in-chief and two others, with a pair of rifles among them. They moved carefully over the rough terrain, trying to live off the land—eating cane, wild plants, and crabs.

Fidel found his brother Raúl and four others on December 17. It was a joyful reunion and, according to the resulting legend, set off Fidel's irrepressible optimism. "We have won the war!" he exulted. At least the situation was getting no worse.

In the next few days, more of the rebels came together. A new ally, Cresencio Pérez, made this happen. Pérez, an old bandit leader of the Sierra Maestra, ruled the lives of thousands of peasants over a vast territory. He had no love for the established government and was willing to throw in his lot with the rebels for the possibility of future considerations. Pérez's help in reuniting the rebels, guiding them, and arranging for supplies was invaluable. The old man, a common criminal by all accounts, became a hero of the revolution.

During December 19–20, Peréz brought other members of the *Granma* expedition, including Che Guevara, to the peasant farmhouse where Fidel waited. How many were rejoined is difficult to say exactly because of conflicting reports by those who were there. Fidel liked to speak of "the twelve" because of its significance in the lore of Christianity. The number invited identification with Jesus Christ and his disciples. Fidel used this comparison to good advantage in creating a mythology for the revolution. Fidel-Christ and his twelve bearded apostles had come to save Cuba, if not the world. In a country where orthodox Christianity and ancient superstition met and intermingled, it was a useful analogy.

On the night of January 15–16, their ranks having swelled to thirty or so with the addition of peasant volunteers, the rebels attacked a small army outpost. The La Plata barracks fell after a short fight. The modest victory showed that, as a fighting unit, the rebels could take a military objective. It was also Fidel's first success as a military leader after a series of notable failures—Moncada, the abortive *Granma* landing, and the rout at Alegría del Pío. If Fidel was going to be a successful revolutionary leader, he had to go beyond enthusiasm, optimism, and a lot of bold talk to achieve success as a military strategist. La Plata increased his stature. It also added to the meager rebel store of guns, ammunition, and supplies.

The world knew little of what was happening with Fidel Castro in the Sierra Maestra. During the Christmas to New Year period, the 26 July Movement maintained pressure on the Batista government with small attacks and bombings of public places. Publicity over the reprisals which followed—torture, shootings, and hangings—created sympathy for the revolutionaries.

The urban wing of M-26-7 and the other groups which cooperated with it knew virtually nothing about the fate of their leader or his men. Through censorship, the government controlled all news of the revolution in progress and printed nothing detri-

Fidel Castro (**upper left**) *with his high school basketball team. Fidel was a star athlete, excelling in basketball, baseball, soccer, track, and swimming.*

Fidel's personal heroes
as a student were
the founder of the
Spanish Fascist party, José
Antonio Primo de Rivera (above),
and the Spanish dictator,
Francisco Franco (at right).

While at the University of Havana, Fidel immersed himself in student politics.

Ramón Grau San Martín, president of Cuba during the time Fidel was a college student and an early target of Fidel's growing political activism.

(Facing page, top) *General Fulgencio Batista, surrounded by Cuban soldiers, staged a bloodless coup with the backing of the Cuban army.* (Facing page, bottom) *The twenty-two Cuban exiles in Mexico City arrested for plotting the overthrow of President Fulgencio Batista. Fidel is standing, the sixth from the right.*

(Above) *Fidel in the high country of the Sierra Maestra Mountains, home for his revolutionary band*

(Inset) *Ernesto "Che" Guevara, a member of the*
inner circle around Fidel.
Fidel watches one of his revolutionary soldiers
test a rifle in the Sierra Maestra Mountains.

*Fidel and his soldiers needed the support
and help of Cuban farmers to continue their
revolution. Here Castro stopped to talk with
a farmer during a tour of the foothills
of the Sierra Maestra Mountains.*

(Facing page, top) *Two truckloads of Cuban soldiers cross a stream while climbing a winding mountain road in search of Fidel and his revolutionaries.* (Facing page, bottom) *Fidel Castro, Jr., "Fidelito," with some of his father's revolutionary soldiers.* (Above) *Revolutionary troops paraded through downtown Havana in a show of strength.*

*The revolution has succeeded—Fidel and his troops
raise their hands in salute at a giant rally in front of
the presidential palace in Havana in January 1959.*
(Inset) *Fidel speaks to the press with his
brother Raúl about reports of a military
revolt against the new revolutionary regime.*

Fidel reads the oath of office upon being sworn in as prime minister of Cuba in 1959. He appealed to Cubans to be patient about reforms and to "aid and understand us."
(Inset) *On Castro's tour of the United States, Canada, Argentina, Brazil, and Uruguay, he held many news conferences such as the one pictured here in Brazil.*

*Fidel and his followers installed themselves
in the Hotel Teresa in Harlem during their visit
to New York City in 1960.*

A jovial meeting took place between Fidel and Nikita Khrushchev after Fidel addressed the United Nations in late 1960.

Headlines in late 1960 announce President John F. Kennedy's naval blockade of Cuba, an action in response to the presence of Russian offensive missiles in Cuba.

Still a powerful figure, Fidel speaks
to the United Nations in 1979.

*Because of fuel shortages, Castro purchased 200,000
bicycles to be used by Cubans as transportation
instead of buses and cars.*

*Castro today: at the 1991 ceremony to honor troops
returning from Angola, and (inset) congratulating U.S.
rower Peggy Johnson after presenting her with a gold
medal at the 1991 Pan American Games held in Cuba.*

mental to its own cause. In a program of disinformation, Batista denied at first that there were any rebels in Cuba. Forced to admit that the rebels did exist, he then reported that Fidel and Raúl had been killed at Alegría del Pío. Hearing the radio reports, Fidel knew that he had to spread the good news that he and the revolution were very much alive. He needed publicity.

At the end of January, Fidel sent a messenger to Havana to locate a foreign correspondent willing to meet with him. The *New York Times* sent one of its most experienced reporters, Herbert Matthews, to cover the story of the fledgling Cuban revolution. For Fidel it was a fortunate choice.

Herbert Matthews was a respected war correspondent familiar with trouble spots all over the world. He was also, maintains Georgie Anne Geyer, a "hopeless romantic" attracted to high-minded causes.[2] The chemistry between the two men would be just right for Fidel's purposes. They met at dawn, at a campsite in the foothills of the Sierra Maestra. Matthews was captivated and began to weave the account, soon to become legend, of the heroic mountain fighter in the cause of freedom.

> The personality of the man is overpowering. It was easy to see that his men adored him. . . . Here was an educated, dedicated fanatic, a man of ideals, of courage and of remarkable qualities of leadership . . . one got a feeling that he is now invincible.[3]

The series of articles Matthew published in the *New York Times*—the first appeared on February 24—made Fidel Castro an international figure and gave him invaluable and much-needed publicity at home.

Fidel used Matthews to paint a much rosier picture of the progress of the revolution than the facts warranted. He cleverly exaggerated the extent of his support and strength. During the interview, Raúl marched the same group of men back and forth through the camp to convey the impression of a large and bustling military organization, rather than the reality of a tired force of twenty to thirty men hanging on to a mountain. A photograph of the reporter standing next to Fidel was published with Matthews's article. It embarrassed the Batista government, which had been claiming all along that Fidel was dead. Because of Matthews's article, sympathy for Fidel Castro rose as support for Batista declined. This brilliant publicity coup, coupled with the public outcry over the excesses of the Batista government, swelled the ranks of revolutionary supporters in Cuba.

Made to look foolish by Castro's recent publicity and its own inability to stop him, the Batista government moved more military units into the Sierra Maestra. The plan was to create a barrier across the province through which supplies and reinforcements could not reach the rebels. In theory, Batista should have been able to accomplish this. He had at his disposal a 40,000-soldier army, supported by a modern air force and navy. American military officers had trained some of its units. The United States was also Cuba's number-one weapons supplier, selling Batista large quantities of airplanes, tanks, armored troop carriers, artillery, bombs, rockets, and small arms. In terms of all the military hardware labeled "Made in America," the U.S. had a strong presence in the events of the Cuban revolution. But weapons alone don't make an army. The Cuban military, like the Cuban government, was far from being a well-oiled and smooth-running machine. It was plagued by dissension, corruption, and incompetence. The man at the top, Fulgencio Batista, could not or did not put together the right combination of will and effective leadership to squash the tiny band of rebels in the mountains. Compounding his problems, he continued to underestimate the strength and resolve of his enemy.

While the army tried to corner its elusive prey in the Sierra Maestra, things were heating up in Havana with more acts of sabotage and terrorism against the government. Much of this took place independently of Fidel's 26 July Movement. University students, members of the Directorio Revolucionario, and fighters under the banner of ex-president Prío all mounted violent and aggressive campaigns against the Batista government. All believed they had an important role to play in any new Cuban government created by the revolution. All represented competition for Fidel Castro.

Under the leadership of José Echeverría, the Directorio devised a bold and desperate plan to attack the presidential palace in Havana and assassinate Fulgencio Batista. Successful, it could have stolen the momentum of leadership from Fidel and M-26-7. Because of a leak in security, the plan was doomed from the beginning. Eighty rebels stormed the palace in broad daylight on March 13. Batista, warned of an impending attack, isolated himself from the rebels on the top floor of the palace. Down below, the grounds soon swarmed with government troops and tanks. The attack sputtered, then collapsed. Thirty-five of the rebels died, including Fidel's potential rival, José Echeverría. Fidel branded the enterprise "a useless expenditure of blood."

There was a backlash from the abortive coup. The action created widespread sympathy for Batista among Cuban and foreign business leaders and members of the upper class. A heavy-handed reaction followed—more arrests, more torture and disappearances.

Though the attempt on his life may have earned Batista sympathy from temporary allies, it eventually brought to the revolution more dedicated converts, especially among the young. For every revolutionary the government murdered without trial, many more new fighters joined the cause. Thus, the Batista government hastened its own demise.

From Fidel in the Sierra a lifeline extended to Frank País, who headed the urban action groups in Santiago. Isolated in the Sierra, the rebels depended on their city brothers for reinforcements, supplies— especially vitally needed weaponry—and information. País believed the struggle in the cities to be as important, perhaps more so, than Fidel's work in the Sierra. He certainly believed it to be more difficult and dangerous and even joked about going to the Sierra for a vacation. País and Castro argued continually about how vital but meager resources should be allocated between the groups. Fidel disliked the arguing as much as he hated his dependence on País.

Frank País sent Fidel's first reinforcements— fifty men from Santiago—in June 1957. Fidel now regrouped the eighty men under his command into three units led by Raúl, Jorge Sostús, and Juan Almeida. His own headquarters group included Che as doctor and Universo Sánchez as chief of staff. Celia Sánchez also joined the staff about this time.

Sánchez, twenty-nine when she first met Fidel, sought him out in the Sierra Maestra. For some time a member of the anti-Batista resistance, she served Fidel first as a courier, moving valuable intelligence in and out of the mountains. Soon she became one of the most important people in Fidel's life, certainly his most trusted and faithful supporter. As a combination personal and business manager, she supervised the details of Fidel's existence and kept the books for a revolution. She had a special knack for dealing with the often temperamental Fidel. Celia was one of the few who could be openly critical of him and get away with it. Raúl and Che were the others, but even they had to tread lightly. Fidel Castro was not a man who easily listened to others.

Fidel's plan for the spring of 1957 was to avoid direct attacks on army outposts in favor of creating a trustworthy support network among the local peasants, no easy task because of the constant risk of betrayal by government informers. Earlier in the year one such informer, Eutimio Guerra, infiltrated the rebel group. He not only passed on information about rebel positions but came close to assassinating Fidel, prevented only by a lack of courage. The rebels uncovered Guerra's treachery and shot him. This was also the fate of the other spies and informers tempted to betrayal by large sums of army money. Most of the local peasants were helpful and loyal to the cause of the revolution. Fidel took pains, from the time of the *Granma* landing, to treat the peasants with respect. Whenever possible, the rebels paid fair prices for food and supplies and did not harass the women. Fidel's policy paid off. He could not have survived in the Sierra without the support of the peasants, who would always claim a special relationship with their *líder máximo*.

After the Matthews interview, other foreign correspondents worked their way into the Sierra to find Fidel and his *barbudos* (bearded ones). When CBS correspondents Robert Taber and Wendell Hoffman located him, Fidel put on his most moderate and reasonable face for the camera. He portrayed himself as a man opposed to bloodshed who was forced into it by the evil of the Batista government. In the film interview, which was well-received by its American audience, Fidel repledged his allegiance to the democratic constitution of 1940. He also urged the United States government to halt its arms shipments to Batista on the grounds that American bullets and bombs were being used against the Cuban people. The interview enhanced Fidel's image in America, a land always fond of heroes and underdogs. Fidel knew how to milk for all it was worth the image of the bearded warrior fighting for the noble cause. He was, and is, a showman.

Basing their views on these few reports, Americans may have tended to romanticize the life of the rebels in the Sierra Maestra. The reality of their life was hard. Food was scarce and monotonous: one meal a day, mostly local vegetables and rice, occasionally some chicken; on rare days a roast pig. Living conditions were Spartan. The men slept in hammocks of their own making. The work of soldiering, often marching long hours in rain and mud or moving up and down across the mountainous terrain, taxed bodies and shoe leather. Medical attention was marginal and dependent on scarce supplies. Even the rebel doctor, Che Guevara, was often so sick with his own asthma that he could not tend to the others. Dentistry was in the hands of amateurs. Fidel once complained to Celia Sánchez that his teeth hurt so badly that he could not think straight.

The rebels—mostly men, but also a few women— who survived the rigors of mountain living were those with fire in their bellies, the dedication to a cause which gave them a higher purpose. Many who came did not stay because of the harsh conditions. Keeping a regular fighting force was a huge problem for Fidel and his cadre of officers. Only leaders like Martí and Fidel Castro had the charisma and vision to hold guerrilla fighters to a purpose under such difficult circumstances.

If life in the Sierra was hard, it was also dangerous. At the end of May the rebels took the offensive. A force of eighty Fidelistas attacked the army outpost at El Uvero. Fidel signaled the start of the assault by opening fire with his telescopic rifle. After a hard fight, the fifty-two-man garrison surrendered. The rebels lost six of their own. It was the costliest engagement of the war thus far in terms of casualties. It was also the most successful for the amount of military hardware—machine guns, rifles, and vehicles—it brought to the movement.

The battle marked a turning point for the rebels. Years later, Fidel said of El Uvero that it had shown them all how to overcome fear and taught them that "the weapons for [their] own victory were in the hands of the enemy." Fidel believed that El Uvero marked the beginning of victory for the revolution.[4]

Though the campaign of the Sierra was hard, that in the cities was in most respects more difficult. The revolution's two fronts—the mountains and the cities—were both important to the success of the movement. It was the urban struggle which was decisive, because it provided the most direct challenge to the Batista government. The loss of life in the cities was far greater than that inflicted in the Sierra Maestra. The suffering was also greater. The rebels of the Sierra could launch an attack, then melt back into the countryside for safety. The city fighters had nowhere to escape and felt the brunt of the government's retaliation for the bombings and assassinations.

Thousands of people, many of them children, were arrested, beaten, and subjected to hideous tortures at the hands of ruthless police and soldiers.

71

Many of the urban fighters risked their lives each day and had few weapons with which to defend themselves. Seldom could they experience any sense of achievement or victory.

Carlos Franqui, one of the key men around Fidel and a fighter in the Sierra Maestra, believed that the leader never paid proper tribute to the role played by the revolutionaries of the city. "Those underground years in the city were a world of crime and horror, an anonymous struggle that swept Cubans into the anti-Batista resistance."[5] It was this force, maintained Franqui, which brought down the government of Fulgencio Batista.

For Fidel the urban wing of the revolution, aside from the Batista government itself, was the greatest threat to his ascendancy to the leadership of the new Cuba he envisioned, however unclear that future may have been during the fighting. Fidel needed to be in total control. The urban guerrillas were largely outside his control for a number of reasons: for a long time he was physically removed from the cities; many of the revolutionary groups were independent of the 26 July Movement; and Frank País, whom Fidel had designated to be leader of the M-26-7 action groups working in the cities, did not always toe the Fidel line.

País often disagreed with his leader and told him so. He may have even distrusted Fidel's motives. He certainly distrusted the Communists close to Fidel— Che and Raúl. País was not about to overthrow one kind of dictatorship so that another could assume its place. Frank País had a large and dedicated personal following among city dwellers. It gave him a base of power independent of Fidel. His contribution to the eventual success of the revolution was every bit as important as that of Fidel Castro.

The United States, in its own curious way, also played a role in the demise of Batista's dictatorship. The United States had approved of Batista's seizure of power. U.S. policy in Cuba had long been shaped by the attitudes of American business interests there. Whatever was good for United Fruit or Standard Oil or most any other Yankee-owned company in Cuba was considered good for America.

America decided it could do business with Batista. He spoke their language. He bought their weaponry. He fought their enemies, the Communists. Castro, on the other hand, was an upstart whose motives and intentions were largely unknown and therefore suspect. The U.S. Ambassador to Cuba, Arthur Gardner, became a close friend of Batista's. He had little use for Castro and suggested that the CIA could infiltrate the Sierra Maestra and assassinate him. Batista refused the offer.

Despite Gardner's enthusiasm for Batista, the official position of Washington on events in Cuba became more and more ambivalent as the war went on. U.S. politicians did not want to appear as though they supported an oppressive dictatorship over a popular and democratic revolutionary movement. Washington sought neutrality. This pleased neither side in Cuba.

Batista felt that he was being let down by an ally with whom he had cooperated fully in the past. From Fidel's point of view, the United States was far from neutral. America was an imperialist country which had for a long time controlled much of the wealth of Cuba through foreign investment and ownership. Of more pressing concern, American bombers, tanks, and guns were killing his people in their fight against the dictatorship of Batista.

Fidel suppressed his hatred of the Yankees when

talking to foreign correspondents. His associates knew his real feelings. To Celia Sánchez he wrote of seeing the effects of weapons from America:

> ... When I saw the rockets they fired at Mario's house, I swore that the Americans would pay dearly for what they are doing here. When this war is over I shall begin a longer and greater war: the war I'll wage against them. I realize that this is my true destiny.[6]

Even with his superior weapons and greater numbers, Batista could not get to the rebels or blockade them. By mid-summer 1967, they controlled a large portion of the Sierra Maestra through which they could move freely, except for an occasional attack by air. Fidel set up a semi-permanent camp, a base of operations, hidden away in a remote valley. The camp had a repair shop, hospital, shoe factory, and an armory. In time there would even be schools and a lecture hall. Rebel numbers in the Sierra had grown to about 200 active fighters. Fidel's biggest problem was not finding new soldiers, but arming them properly.

Frank País was well aware of Fidel's problems and did his best to provide arms, supplies, and replacements. But País had his own problems. Santiago was the crucible of urban revolt in Oriente Province. Under continuous government pressure it was becoming increasingly difficult for M-26-7 to carry out its attacks and acts of sabotage. País lacked the freedom of movement Fidel had won in the Sierra. He soon hoped to leave the city and open a second front in the mountains. He waited too long.

On July 30, 1957, in a back alley of Santiago, Frank País was shot in the back and killed by a government assassin. Thousands of supporters turned out for the funeral of the man whose fame as a hero of the 26 July Movement rivaled that of Fidel in the eyes of many. From his Sierra base, Fidel used País's death as a call to arms. "After seeing the assassination of Frank País, the most courageous, useful, and extraordinary of all our fighters," Fidel broadcast from the Sierra, "what is holding back the thousands of Cubans anxious to do something? . . . The hour has come for all of those who call themselves revolutionaries . . . to put an end to childish dreams." [7]

Frank País's death was a greater loss to the revolution than it was to Fidel personally. For him it meant the elimination of another potential rival for control of the revolutionary movement. No longer would he have to argue about the preeminence of the Sierra Maestra campaign or what shape the revolution should take as it moved toward a post-Batista future. Soon after País's death Fidel wrote to Celia Sánchez, "Our motto from now on should be: All rifles, all bullets, all supplies for the Sierra!" [8]

By the end of 1957, the government proclaimed that Fidel Castro was worth $100,000 dead or alive. But he always seemed just out of reach in his mountain kingdom. The rebels had consolidated their control over 2,000 square miles of Oriente Province. Their army had grown to a modest 300, though foreign correspondents were reporting numbers anywhere between 1,000 and 2,000.

Fidel's political program was still the rather vague reform plan he had outlined in the "History Will Absolve Me" speech and reiterated in the manifestos issued from exile in Mexico. In July, Fidel had co-signed the "Sierra Maestra Manifesto" with Raúl Chibás and Felipe Pazos representing Cuban opposition forces in exile. The purpose of the document was to create a united front among "all opposition political parties, all civic institutions, and all revolutionary forces."

In the manifesto, Fidel agreed to work with the other groups as an equal partner, to turn over the government to a mutually chosen provisional president until free elections could be held, to ensure in any future government that the military should not wield political power, and to support a program of social and political reform. For Fidel, the manifesto was a compromise he had to make for the sake of his revolutionary objectives but one he had no intention of honoring. Fidel was a true Machiavellian, the leader who would say or do anything to further his own agenda. His signature on the manifesto was a deceit and a fraud. Che summed it up:

> We knew that it was a minimum program, a program which limited our effort, but we also knew that it was impossible to establish our will from the Sierra Maestra and that we had to work for a long time with all kinds of "friends" who tried to exploit our military strength and the great confidence which the people already felt for Fidel, for their own macabre ends—above all, to maintain the domination of imperialism in Cuba. . . .[9]

Clearly the *Sierra Manifesto* was a sop to Fidel's temporary allies and nowhere hinted at the radical changes Fidel would later impose on Cuba.

To quell fears about his own role in a new Cuban government, Fidel announced that, after the fall of Batista, Judge Manuel Urrutia would become the provisional president of Cuba until free elections could be held. It was an inspired choice. Urrutia was a moderate and something of a political nonentity. He was a threat to no one and therefore acceptable to everyone. The other members of the "united front" were alarmed that Fidel had made this decision on his own. It was an omen of things to come.

As 1958 unfolded, the Batista government began to unravel under increased revolutionary pressure.

More guerrilla groups formed, operating in the north of Oriente and in the Escambray mountains of Las Villas Province. Fidel stepped up the propaganda war with the creation of a newspaper, *Cubana Libre*, and broadcasts from *Radio Rebelde* in the Sierra Maestra. More strikes erupted, including that of 75,000 schoolchildren. The government responded to stepped-up revolutionary violence with more violence of its own. The bodies of captured rebels hung from trees outside villages and towns to serve as a warning to those who would oppose the government.

In mid-March, pursuing its policy of neutrality, the United States suspended arms shipments to Cuba. Batista felt deserted by his old ally. Embattled and embittered, he resolved to get rid of Fidel Castro once and for all.

The government launched an all-out offensive into the Sierra Maestra in May 1958. Seventeen battalions of soldiers, supported by tank companies, the air force, and the navy, attempted to isolate and squeeze the rebels into a small pocket of the mountains. The campaign failed miserably. Army casualties were high. Morale among the troops hit bottom. Many defected to the rebel cause. The army seemed helpless against the rebels.

Raúl Castro, at the head of a second front in the Sierra Cristal mountains of northern Oriente, further humiliated the government by kidnapping dozens of foreign nationals—U.S. and Canadian workers and U.S. military personnel stationed at Guantánamo. All were eventually released unharmed. The action demonstrated the inability of the Batista government to guarantee anyone's safety. In Oriente Province, at least, the rebels appeared to be in charge of events. Suffering repeated failures, the army withdrew its forces from the Sierra Maestra.

The revolution gained momentum. Fidel devised

plans to come down from the mountains and push westward toward Havana. He divided the rebel army into three strike forces. Fidel, at the head of the main column, would encircle Santiago. Camilo Cienfuegos would leapfrog to the westernmost province, Piñar del Rio. Che Guevara would lead the third force into the center, the province of Las Villas, to sever east-west communications and take control of other rebel groups in the area. It was a clever plan. The net began to close around Batista.

If the dictator did not see where events were heading, officials in Washington could. U.S. interests in Cuba would be best served if Batista stepped down in favor of a new and democratic leadership. Ambassador Smith urged Batista to leave, inviting him to live in the United States.

As Christmas approached, Fulgencio Batista at last made plans to save himself, his family, and a few close associates. He evacuated his children on December 29. Then, after bidding farewell to his supporters at a glum New Year's gathering, he deserted them and flew to the Dominican Republic on January 1, 1959. It was the end and the beginning.

There was effectively no government in Cuba. In the cities, urban rebels of M-26-7 and the Directorio moved into police stations and maintained order on the streets. Few Cubans resorted to violence and looting. The rebels began to assert control.

On January 1–2 Che marched into Havana. Manuel Urrutia became provisional president of Cuba. Camilo Cienfuegos and a 700-man force occupied the large Camp Columbia military installation.

Back in Oriente, Fidel accepted the surrender of Santiago. A carnival atmosphere consumed the city as the rebels entered. Women rushed up to the rebel soldiers, touching and kissing their dirty beards. Fidel personally accepted the surrender of the Moncada barracks, where the revolution had almost foundered five-and-a-half years earlier. He proclaimed that this city, which had been the crucible of revolution throughout the country's history, would be the new capital of Cuba. It was Fidel flexing his muscles. He demonstrated clearly to his shocked revolutionary allies that power was not in Havana or anywhere else except where he was. From his experiences near Fidel before and after the revolutionary victory of 1959, Carlos Franqui observed, "Power never eluded him, and he always managed not to share it." [10]

A tide of Fidel worship began to take hold of Cuba. The January 4 edition of *Revolución* carried a large photo of Fidel Castro on its front page. The caption read, "The Hero-Guide of Cuban Reform. May God continue to illuminate him." Surrounded by cheering and adoring crowds in Santiago, and flanked by his bearded revolutionaries from the mountains, Fidel left that city for Havana. More crowds, more adoration from the masses en route slowed his progress. He was in no hurry. Havana could wait. He toured the countryside, making speeches, meeting the press, and everywhere accepting the tribute of *las mases*.

On January 8 Fidel made his triumphal entry into Havana carrying his now-famous telescopic rifle. His son Fidelito was at his side. He stopped at the presidential palace to confer with Urrutia, then spoke to the people. Carlos Franqui remembered: "From the balcony of the palace he asked the multitudes to open a path: 'The people are my bodyguard.' And like Moses parting the waters, he crossed the sea of people that ran from Misiones Avenue to the bay, a hero out of Greek mythology. . . ." [11] The crowds chanted FIDEL!FIDEL!FIDEL!FIDEL!FIDEL! over and over again. As he addressed the masses below him, two white doves flew up over the gathering. Incredibly, one landed on Fidel's shoulder and remained there as he spoke. It was like a visitation of the Holy Spirit and must have seemed to those assembled a sure sign of God's favor.

CHAPTER FIVE

BUILDING
A
NEW
CUBA

In an explosive outpouring of pent-up emotion, Cubans everywhere rallied to the red and black colors of the revolution and its leader, Fidel Castro. The ranks of the Fidelistas swelled from the few hundred of the Sierra Maestra days to many thousands in the last weeks of the fight against Batista. The revolution that had been promised to the Cuban people for so long, and then denied them by a succession of corrupt political regimes, now seemed to be a reality. Fidel Castro was the embodiment of that revolution. It was as if the great national hero Martí had been reborn in the person of the tall, scraggly-bearded young man in the rumpled olive-green uniform. How they cheered their new hero when he came down from the mountains leading his army of *barbudos*. Expectations soared. Everything would be set right. All things were now possible.

Fidel rode the adulation of the masses gently, modestly, and cleverly. He expressed no personal ambitions beyond serving as the agent of the people.

Power did not interest him. "We are immune to ambitions and vanities," he told the people, as he would tell them many times. Yes, he would accept a temporary role as commander-in-chief of the armed forces. Then, once the government was securely in the hands of democratically elected civilian leaders, he would fade into the background, his work finished. That was the impression he gave.

The organization of a provisional government in January 1959 took place in an atmosphere of hope, comradeship, and enthusiasm. Judge Manuel Urrutia took his place as provisional president. Serving as prime minister was Doctor Miró Cardona, a distinguished lawyer with a record of opposition to Batista. The members of the cabinet—overseeing finance, transportation, education, and such—were a blend of liberal leaders of good reputation and prominent leaders of the rebel army. It seemed a collection of decent and honest people, a rarity in the history of Cuban government.

In the first weeks of the new government, Fidel stayed in the background of government activity. Though he attended none of the early cabinet meetings, he manipulated people and events through several ministers who regularly consulted with him. At no time did Fidel relinquish the authority and power he brought with him into Havana at the head of the revolutionary army.

Though Fidel was a power behind the scenes from the beginning, he did not at first impose a revolutionary program on the Cuban government. At this point it was unlikely that he had a program that went beyond the broad ideas for change voiced earlier at the Moncada trial and in the Sierra Maestra. Making a revolution to topple a government was one thing; creating a suitable replacement was quite another. Everyone had some ideas, but no one had a master plan.

In the midst of a lot of nationalistic, anti-imperialistic, anti-capitalistic slogans being tossed around in January 1959, there seemed to be no definite agreement about what the revolution really stood for. Among members of the government there was a mixed bag of political ideas. Some of the liberals envisioned a new Cuba much like the old, but where free enterprise and a democratic government created social programs to aid the lower classes. The Marxists, like Raúl Castro and Che Guevara, had much more radical changes in mind. They saw a Cuba free of United States influence, a new socialist country—a dictatorship of the proletariat—of which Karl Marx had preached.

But what did Fidel have in mind? No one really knew. Fidel was not in the habit of confiding in others, even his close associates. One of them, Carlos Franqui, complained, ". . . neither I nor anyone else knew Fidel's real ideas." [1]

As the new government began settling in during January, little real work toward building the new Cuba was accomplished. Dealing with the old Batista Cuba held everyone's attention. Every day, newspapers uncovered new evidence of corruption in the former government. Then came the detailed and shocking reports of arrests, torture, and killings by Batista's secret police and military. The dirt that had lain under the rug for so long was now exposed. The more people read, the more they demanded justice and revenge.

Police across the country, acting under the orders of Fidel Castro, arrested hundreds of ex-soldiers, policemen, and civil servants and charged them with what the new government called war crimes. In the early days of January, many of them were shot after quick courts martial. Later, others faced more elaborate trials. Most of the people punished were the small fry of the Batista government. The big fish had been able to use their money to escape the country as the government crumbled. Soon the executions of war criminals became a spectator sport with thousands jamming stadiums to see the firing squads carry out their violent labors.

The executions brought protests from the United States. Fidel answered that the Yankees who had nothing to say in defense of Cubans tortured and killed by Batista had no right to criticize lawful revolutionary justice. How, he asked, could a government who killed hundreds of thousands with atomic bombs at Hiroshima and Nagasaki have the temerity to protest the elimination of a few hundred war criminals?

Again Fidel went directly to the people for support. In a speech before a large crowd in January, he asked all those in favor of revolutionary justice to raise their arms. A forest of arms shot up. Cries of "To the wall!" rang out from the crowd. "The jury of a million Cubans of all ideas and all social classes has voted," announced Fidel.[2]

Fidel continued to speak for the revolution. In fact, he behaved as if he, not Cardona, was the prime minister. And it was true. Cardona was a figurehead, a bit of window decoration to demonstrate how respectable the revolution really was. Fidel was the shaker and mover. No one in the government doubted it, and no one spoke out against him, at least publicly, as Fidel consolidated his power.

As commander-in-chief of the armed forces, Fidel reorganized the military. In the provinces he gave control of the army to rebel officers who had served him well. Pedro Díaz Lanz, who had flown arms to the rebels in the Sierra Maestra, was named chief of Cuba's air force. The military was firmly under Fidel's thumb.

Fidel's position in the revolution was so secure that he flew to Caracas on January 22 to help Venezuelans celebrate the anniversary of the expulsion of their own dictator, Marcos Pérez Jiménez. He also went to thank them for their financial support of the Cuban revolution. A large, enthusiastic crowd cheered his arrival at the airport. It was the first of many such outpourings of feeling Fidel would receive from the people, if not the leaders, of Latin America.

At home, Fidel's popularity "bordered on madness," in the words of Carlos Franqui. *El Commandante* (The Major), as Fidel was widely and fondly known, continued his seduction of the masses, both in personal appearances around the country and on television, which he used to great advantage. These were his "conversations with his people." For their part, while his people may not have understood where he was headed, they put their faith in the *líder máximo* to do the right thing. It was a blind faith.

The Camelot atmosphere of January began to dissipate in February as Fidel took more direct control of governance. As long as the revolutionary program remained rather vague and undefined, members of the government who embraced different political views could cooperate or at least seem to cooperate with one another. As Fidel began to define the revolution, to take it down a more radical path than had been expected, people began to squirm.

Seeing no political futures for themselves in the government that seemed to be evolving, both Urrutia and Cardona tried to resign in February over policy differences with Fidel. Urrutia stayed in office according to Fidel's wish, but Cardona was allowed to depart. The cabinet offered the vacant office of prime minister to Fidel. He had the power, he might as well accept the title. Fidel agreed, but only if the cabinet granted him broad powers "in order to carry forward the revolutionary program." The cabinet, with little will of its own, readily acceded to this demand and modified the constitution of 1940 to allow for the necessary changes. This was the same constitution to which Fidel had pledged his undying support in the Moncada trial speech.

With this new assumption of power, Fidel pushed provisional president Urrutia into the background with little to do but formally sign bills into law. Urrutia's time was quickly drawing to a close. Fidel's previous title of commander-in-chief of the armed forces went to his brother, Raúl.

Cabinet meetings clearly showed Fidel was in charge and was not disposed to share power. The number of meetings decreased and little of importance took place when they were held. Often, Fidel kept ministers waiting for hours until he joined them in his own good time. Then he discouraged any free exchange of ideas on matters of policy. Outside the intermittent meetings, Fidel was elusive. He had no fixed living place, but alternated between the home of Celia Sánchez, a suite at the Havana Hilton, and a rented place outside the city. Often, cabinet members simply couldn't find him. As a result, a paralysis set in on decision making. Things happened only when Fidel wanted them to happen. "This train," he announced mysteriously, "knows where it is going." Just where that was, only Fidel understood. His power came from the people, and Fidel believed that only he really knew what the people wanted. He has remained firm in that assertion over the years. "It is my understanding that my influence flows from a correct interpretation of the needs and aspirations and the possibilities of the people and from correct interpretation of what things had to be done."[3] Early on, Fidel used his popular mandate to attack what he saw as the big problems of a sick Cuban economic system: the unequal distribution of wealth, the dependence of the economy on sugar, and the dominance of the United States in Cuban economic affairs.

While Cuba seemed a prosperous nation compared to others in Latin America, most of that prosperity had always been controlled and enjoyed by a minority at the top. It seemed there were two Cubas, one rich and one poor. The people of the rich Cuba lived in large houses on big estates or in the affluent suburbs of Havana. They enjoyed private beaches, sent their children to be educated in the United States, and went shopping in Miami and New York at Christmas time.

Most people lived in the poor Cuba. They were often out of work, lived in miserable shacks, and had little opportunity for good education or decent health care. Fidel knew both Cubas. His family was rich, but it lived surrounded by the poor cane cutters and small farmers of Oriente Province. He had come to know them first hand during his campaign in the Sierra Maestra, and had promised them economic justice when the revolution succeeded.

Part of the reason why such an inequity in the distribution of wealth existed in Cuba was because of the country's dependence on sugar. Columbus introduced sugarcane cultivation into the New World, and Cuba's soil conditions were especially suited to it. In time Cuba became the "sugar bowl" of the world, producing between a third and a half of all sugar consumed. Her biggest customer was the United States of America which, under a sugar quota, agreed to purchase the bulk of the Cuban harvest each year. Sugar continues to dominate Cuba's economy, accounting for 90 percent of its income and 80 percent of all exports.

The country experienced serious social and economic costs due to the sugar monoculture. In their early attempts to develop the island, the Spanish enslaved and largely destroyed Cuba's native Indian population. Spain then introduced African slaves in 1517 to provide the labor necessary for planting and harvesting. The importation of slaves kept pace with labor needs until slavery was abolished in the 1880s. Afro-Cubans were and, long after slavery was ended, continued to be the poorest of Cuba's poor. Cubans of African descent, listed either as black or mulatto (mixed race), now make up about 62 percent of the total population.

People in control of production made fortunes when sugar prices were up. Many became millionaires. When prices were down, the workers at the bottom of society suffered the most. Prices fluctuated enormously over the years, and Cuba's prosperity and the well-being of her people went up and down with the changes.

Workers were the biggest victims of sugar production. Even in the best of times, labor was seasonal. Cane cutters sweated away feverishly in the fields for four months at low wages, then were unemployed for much of the rest of the year. Even after slavery was officially abolished in Cuba, workers remained slaves to the system of sugar production.

Fidel knew sugar. It had made the Castro family fortune. He also understood Cuba's unhealthy dependence on this single crop and believed that the revolution provided the opportunity needed to diversify her economy. He also understood that Cuba's dependence on sugar was a dependence on the United States of America. Americans were both the owners of the Cuban sugar industry and its major customers.

Through most of its modern history, the Cuban economy, and much of its way of life, was dominated by the Yankee colossus to the north. By the middle of the nineteenth century, America was Cuba's most important trading partner. Americans bought most of the annual Cuban sugar production and manufactured most of the goods imported into the country. U.S. investment made Cuba an economic dependent of American business and banking interests. American money controlled utilities, the rail system, banks, cattle ranches, sugar and oil refineries, and mining production. By 1959 American investment in Cuba was $1 billion, more than in any other Latin American nation except Venezuela. Economic power ensured political power. It was often said that Fulgencio Batista was the second most powerful man in the country—next to the American ambassador.

Fidel took on the problems of the Cuban economy the way he started the revolution, counting on enthusiasm and right-headedness to take the place of experience. Not a trained economist, he was ill-equipped to understand and decide upon policies whose effects would reach far into the future. As a result, he bumped along from week to week, year to year, achieving success here and committing colossal blunders there.

In March 1959, he made some changes that had an immediate effect on the distribution of wealth in the country and were immensely popular among "his people," Cubans with low and modest incomes. First he slashed rents 50 percent for all those paying under $100 a month. Since most low income people were renters, this immediately put money in the pockets of those who needed it most. Soon after, Fidel marched on the telephone company, long a target of popular complaint, and cut rates significantly. Then, with much fanfare and publicity, Fidel began to redistribute land to those who before could only dream of owning it. He gave away 25,000 acres (10,121 hectares), land that had been confiscated by the revolutionary government, in the province of Pinar del Río. To each farmer selected for the giveaway, Fidel awarded a plot of about 69 acres (28 hectares).

These changes were popular and easy to accomplish. The resulting enthusiasm made Fidel believe he knew what he was doing. But, he was really flying by the seat of his pants, moving through the unfamiliar territory of economic planning and development. Too often he went for the short-term gain instead of making the hard and perhaps unpopular decisions needed for the long term. When meat prices should have been allowed to rise in response to a decrease in supply, Fidel kept prices low. This gave more meat to "his people" but also resulted in overslaughtering. Even stud cattle were butchered, thus ensuring future shortages.

While it was fairly easy for Fidel to make a few popular changes affecting the distribution of wealth in Cuba, to define a new economic relationship with the United States was much more difficult. Publicly, he maintained a moderate tone toward the United States, at least in the beginning. With the newborn revolution still unsteady on its feet, it was not the time to make enemies. Privately, his anti-American sentiments were as strong as ever. He had not forgotten U.S. support of the Batista government, and he blamed the Yankees for much of what was wrong with Cuba. As disagreement between the two countries grew, it became more difficult for the proud Fidel to maintain his pose of moderation.

Especially irritating was U.S. criticism of Cuba's execution of "enemies of the state," as Fidel called them. Neither did he like the fact that so many exiled Batista "war criminals" had been granted asylum by the U.S. government. This became more of an issue as an active anti-Castro opposition movement began to grow in Miami. The Eisenhower administration was tolerating this threat to the Cuban revolution, Fidel charged, if not aiding it outright.

For its part, Washington grew increasingly alarmed about the Communist influence in Cuba. American conservatives accused Fidel Castro of being a Communist. He denied it. In a report to President Eisenhower, the C.I.A. claimed that Communist or not, Cuba was becoming a dictatorship under Castro. It was in this atmosphere of mistrust that Fidel traveled to the United States in mid-April 1959 at the invitation not of the U.S. government, but the American Society of Newspaper Editors.

Arriving at the airport in Washington, D.C., Fidel looked as if he had just come down from the Sierra Maestra. A cheering crowd gave a warm public reception to the tall, bearded revolutionary in his rumpled and worn green uniform. The official government reception seemed to the Cuban delegation to be much closer to freezing.[4]

Despite the real or imagined chill, Fidel handled himself well. He smiled for the cameras and conveyed a lively moderation in his appearances before audiences in Washington, New York, and at Harvard and Princeton universities. He was even usually on time for his speeches, though keeping his talks short enough was sometimes a problem for the man used to rattling on for hours. Asked to limit his remarks before the National Press Club in Washington to thirty minutes, he kept everyone prisoner for two hours. At each stop he heard variations of the same question. "What about Communist influence in your government?"

The constant references to Communism—what he believed was an obsessive interest—irritated Fidel. Nevertheless, he calmly denied the charges at every turn. "I can tell you clearly," he said to the National Press Club, "we are not Communists." During a street interview, Fidel quipped, "We are not Communists or capitalists. We are Cubanists."

In the middle of Central Park in New York, he proclaimed that the revolution was aiming at a "humanist democracy," which he defined as "human rights with the satisfaction of the needs of man."[5] He also unveiled several slogans which he would return to again and again in the coming months: "No bread without liberty, no liberty without bread" and "Freedom with bread, bread without terror." In addition to denying any Communist connections at a meeting with U.S. Congressmen, he spoke to another of their concerns, the protection of American property and investment. Fidel's ambiguous declaration should have reassured no one. "We have no intention of expropriating U.S. property, and any property we take we'll pay for."[6]

Communism was also a topic of discussion in the only top-level contact Fidel had with the Eisenhower administration. He met with Vice-President Richard Nixon for almost two-and-a-half hours. The two leaders did not hit it off. To Fidel, Nixon was a "son-of-a-bitch" who had treated him badly. Nixon saw Castro as a charismatic amateur "obsessed with the idea that it was his responsibility to carry out the will of the people whatever it might appear to be at a particular time. . . ."[7]

Nixon, with a nose attuned to sniffing out Communists, reportedly told an associate after the meeting with Castro that the Cuban leader was "a Red." He did not go that far in his official report to the president, but emphasized what he saw as Castro's lack of experience in political and economic affairs and his "naive attitude toward communism." The closing words of the report were prophetic.

> Whatever we may think of him he is going to be a great factor in the development of Cuba and very possibly in Latin American affairs generally. He seems to be sincere. He is either incredibly naive about communism or under Communist discipline—my guess is the former, and as I have already implied his ideas as how to run a government or an economy are less developed than those of almost any world figure I have met in fifty countries.
>
> But because he has the power to lead . . . we have no choice but at least to try to orient him in the right direction.[8]

If Fidel was not a big hit with Nixon, he did make a favorable impression on the American people. Compared to the steady, staid, grandfatherly look of their own President Eisenhower, Castro cut a bold, brash, romantic image, like a figure out of the Old West. He was a photographer's dream. The journalists snapped the bearded, cigar-chomping rebel at the zoo, at Yankee Stadium eating the obligatory American hotdog, and everywhere on the streets just talking to ordinary people.

But what did Fidel expect to gain by all this? He surprised both his own advisers and the U.S. government by not asking for American economic aid, though American leaders had previously hinted that such a request would be looked upon favorably. Aid would have been a way to try and "orient him in the right direction," as Nixon recommended. Whether Fidel was playing a waiting game—hoping for a stronger bargaining position in the future—or declaring Cuba's independence from the United States is difficult to say. In any case, his actions would soon cancel all likelihood of economic aid from the U.S. government.

Leaving the United States, Fidel moved on to make appearances in Canada, Argentina, Brazil, and Uruguay. At each stop, he reasserted that Cuba would avoid both capitalism and Communism in favor of a "revolutionary humanism." He coined new slogans. "Ours," he proclaimed, "is a revolution of the poor and for the poor. A revolution as Cuban as our palms. Not a red revolution but an olive-green revolution." [9]

Fidel returned to Havana on May 7, 1959. His three-week excursion had given the revolution some breathing room. It raised his prestige abroad, kept the Yankees guessing, and allowed more time at home for the consolidation of his power. The image of the calm, moderate, and appealing revolutionary that Fidel projected across the Americas defused the criticism of enemies and potential enemies both at home and abroad. Soon after arriving home, he set into motion a huge economic change for Cuba, the Agrarian Reform Law, which moved the revolution into a more radical phase than most had expected it to go. Fidel was full of surprises.

The Agrarian Reform Law continued the program of land redistribution Fidel had begun earlier. It was Fidel's plan all the way, with little input from the cabinet. Since Fidel always liked a show, the final meeting on the bill and its signing into law took place at the old rebel headquarters at La Plata in the Sierra Maestra. Fidel noted, surely tongue in cheek, that the historic surroundings would inspire his ministers. It rained a lot, it was cold, and there wasn't enough food. Officials and journalists trudged up mountain paths for hours to reach the camp. Fidel arrived by helicopter. Everyone slept without blankets on the floors of the old buildings. Thousands of peasants crowded the area to see their beloved Fidel who was giving them land.

The Agrarian Reform Law created a new and powerful institution, the National Institute for Agrarian Reform (INRA). The INRA would henceforth supervise land redistribution and implement agricultural policy across the country. Fidel was its president.

Under the new law, almost 200,000 peasants received land doled out in mimimum holdings of about 67 acres (27 hectares). In most cases, maximum holdings for individuals and corporations were set at 988 acres (400 hectares). The law prohibited foreigners from owning farmland in Cuba. Thus, American-owned sugar mills could not own private cane fields as they had in the past.

Taken at face value, the Agrarian Reform Bill seemed to break up large private estates and give the land to the peasants. In fact, ownership rights were very restricted. First, the land could never be sold or mortgaged. Second, peasants had to grow what they were told and had no control over prices. What the law really did was to put the government of Cuba in the agriculture business by the creation of large cooperative farms supervised by the INRA. At the top of everything was Fidel Castro, Super Farmer, who really knew very little about agriculture but continued to make decisions as if he did.

The passage of the Agrarian Reform Law triggered alarms in both the United States and Cuba. Wasn't this clearly communism? In response to Fidel's claim that the revolution was "olive-green" came new charges. The revolution might be green on the outside, said his critics, but, like a watermelon, it was red on the inside.

Was Fidel a Communist at this time? Answering that question was a popular pastime both inside and outside Cuba. His critics charged he had been a Communist all along, even at the university when he walked around with one of Lenin's books under his arm. If Fidel was a Communist during the years of revolutionary fighting and in the months following the overthrow of Batista, he hid it well. Carlos Franqui, a Communist himself at one time and one of Fidel's intimates, couldn't see it.

> No one thought Fidel was a Communist. I mean no one. We knew that Raúl Castro was a Communist, that Che Guevera was also, and that Camilo, Ramiro, Celia, Haydée, and some commandantes and other collaborators were Communists, too. But no one knew about Fidel, including me—who saw him at quite close range—and even his most intelligent enemies.[10]

Fidel publicly denied being a Communist in 1958 when he first gained some international recognition. He certainly had no high regard for the Communist party in Cuba. It had adopted a policy of co-existence with Batista, who had allowed Communists to head the labor unions. Cuban Communists had condemned Fidel's Moncada attack and his early efforts in the Sierra Maestra. What he was doing did not fit their idea of how a revolution was supposed to take place. Eventually, when the party saw where things were heading, it hopped aboard the revolutionary bandwagon in the last weeks of the Batista regime.

Communists had a role to play in the new government, but in the beginning not a big one. By June of 1959, things had changed. Fidel appeared to be working toward some kind of understanding with his former critics. Eighteen months later, as he moved Cuba into a close alliance with the Soviet Union, he would say emphatically, "I say it with pride and confidence; I am a Marxist-Leninist and I shall be a Marxist-Leninist until the day I die." [11]

In mid-June 1959, however, no one could know that Fidel embraced communism, if in fact he did.

He played one group against the other, giving assurances to both Communists and anti-Communists, depending on which group he happened to be talking to at the moment. Fidel used people, and he used them well to serve his own interests.

As more people became concerned about Fidel's leftist leanings, organized and active opposition to him increased. Counterrevolutionary activity had been going on inside Cuba ever since the fall of the Batista government. Former Batista supporters were operating in the mountains, much as Fidel had done, but with no real success. There was no base of support for such activity. The peasants and city workers were firmly behind Fidel. Sometimes trouble broke out. Three distant bomb explosions punctuated a Castro speech in mid-June. No one took this counterrevolutionary activity too seriously, though Fidel made the most of it for propaganda purposes to unite the Cuban people against "the enemy."

Fidel also faced opposition from within his own government. On June 29, 1959, Pedro Días Lanz, head of the air force, defected to the United States. There he testified to a Senate committee that Cuba was rotten with communism. About this same time, President Manuel Urrutia began making anti-Communist television speeches charging that "Communists are inflicting terrible harm on Cuba." [12]

Fidel used the opportunity to get rid of Urrutia; he had outlived his usefulness to the regime. Cleverly, Fidel resigned, then disappeared for two days. It was another of Fidel's moments of high drama. *Revolución* announced Fidel's resignation in banner headlines on July 15. The country exploded in reaction. Huge demonstrations in support of Fidel broke out everywhere. The country shut down.

After a few days, Fidel went on television and destroyed Urrutia's reputation, accusing him of trying to provoke foreign intervention and of misusing government funds. Urrutia resigned, then sought refuge in the Venezuelan Embassy. Eventually, the former President of Cuba escaped the country disguised as a milkman, another victim of Fidel's ruthlessness.

The cabinet appointed a new president, Osvaldo Dorticós. Actually, it was Fidel's appointment. Dorticós was Fidel's puppet and yes-man. The power belonged to the *Máximo Líder*, as it always had.

The people ratified the changes on July 26 when thousands gathered in the Plaza Cívica to celebrate the sixth anniversary of Moncada. President Dorticós announced to the crowd that Fidel had consented to resume the post of prime minister. The plaza erupted in cheers and cries of *"Viva Fidel!"* The prime minister's speech lasted for four hours and was frequently interrupted with cheering, dancing, and singing. Hawkers snaked through the crowd selling soft drinks, food, and hats. Fidel's direct democracy at work was like carnival.

Fidel enjoyed a strong base of support among peasants, city workers, and the lower middle class. Because much of Cuba's capitalist system was still intact, many individuals and companies were still willing to cooperate with the Castro regime despite the reforms enacted. But not everyone felt that way.

Hardest hit were the big landowners and cattle ranchers who lost land in the agrarian reform. In mid-August, the ranchers set into motion a plot to overthrow Fidel and seize control of the government. The conspiracy—involving 2,000 men and backed by the Trujillo government of the Dominican Republic—fizzled. Government troops arrested and imprisoned most of the conspirators. The failed coup served only to make the Castro regime more security conscious.

The increasingly repressive government response toward real and imagined enemies soon packed the country's jails and prisons fuller than they had been under Batista. Under the pressure, more people left Cuba in search of better economic opportunity and a freer environment. Many of them were technical advisers, planners, and administrators whom the revolution badly needed to rebuild the country. Some joined opposition groups in the United States.

Anti-Castro exiles based in Florida began to launch attacks on Cuba. In October 1959, an aircraft dropped several bombs on a sugar mill in Pinar del Río. Soon after, former air force head Pedro Díaz Lanz returned to Cuba in a B-25, bombing Havana with leaflets charging that Castro was a Communist. The effect of this harassment was a circle-the-wagons mentality that Fidel encouraged. He was always at his best with an enemy to confront. Perhaps he needed one.

Feeling embattled and unable to get armaments from the United States or its allies, Fidel approached the Soviet Union for military supplies. By turning toward the east Fidel showed his back to the United States. The old relationship was becoming increasingly strained, and Fidel was becoming more inclined to reject all things Yankee.

In December 1959, behaving much like Dr. Seuss's Grinch who stole Christmas, Fidel Castro abolished Santa Claus in Cuba. Santa, seen as a decadent, imperialist import from America, became another casualty of Fidelismo. The bearded Fidel, not the bearded Santa Claus, would become the focus of holiday celebrations in Cuba.

CHAPTER SIX

THE
BAD NEIGHBOR POLICY

There was a big New Year's party at the Havana-Libre Hotel to welcome in 1960. Fidel was the center of attention, as usual. His personal guest was a black American, the famous boxer Joe Louis. Louis, a long-time champion, had retired and was a bit punchy from all those years in the ring giving and taking beatings. He was especially remembered for defeating the German champ, Max Schmelling, prior to World War II when Adolf Hitler was spouting a lot of Aryan superiority propaganda. It had not sat well in Germany when Louis, supposedly a member of an "inferior race," had put Schmelling on the canvas. It was the kind of success story that appealed to Fidel, who liked boxers, and who, as an underdog, had just KO'd Fulgencio Batista. Fidel was about to take on an even bigger opponent, the United States of America. There would be a lot of punches and counterpunches in the coming year.

At the beginning of 1960, a balance still existed between moderate and leftist influences in the Cuban government. Fidel was the fulcrum and could tip the balance either way as it suited his purposes. As the year unfolded, the more radical influences began to gain ascendancy, especially as Cuban-American relations deteriorated and Fidel turned eastward toward the Soviet Union. Under growing American criticism and threats to cancel or reduce the sugar quota, Fidel grew increasingly interested in the Soviet Union as a potential friend, ally, and source of assistance. And the Soviets were interested in getting a foothold in the Americas and countering the military strength of its Cold War adversary, the United States.

In early February 1960, the vice-prime minister of the U.S.S.R., Anastas Mikoyan, arrived in Cuba, the first such visit ever by a high-ranking Soviet leader. Fidel rolled out the red carpet. He and Cuba's Communist leaders met Mikoyan at the airport, then whisked him away for a grand tour of the island that lasted for weeks.

As a result of Mikoyan's visit, the Soviet Union agreed to purchase a substantial portion of the Cuban sugar crop for 1960 and the four years following. The Soviets made trade agreements covering other Cuban commodities and also granted several hundred million dollars worth of credits toward the purchase of Soviet raw materials and machinery for new factories. Cuba agreed to purchase large quantities of Russian crude oil. As a result of the new ties with the Soviet Union, Fidel began to gain the independence from the United States he so badly wanted. As the new relationship with the Soviets blossomed, the old one with the United States continued to decline. Fidel seized on events in the coming months to strengthen his position at home and build Cuba's image abroad as a strong and independent nation of consequence.

On March 4, 1960, during the joyous annual celebration of carnival, the French ship *La Coubre*, un-
loading arms and dynamite from Belgium, exploded
in Havana harbor. The port erupted in a huge mush-
room cloud. The massive explosion killed or injured
275 dockworkers and threw the city into confusion
and panic for several hours. Large headlines in *Revolución* immediately proclaimed the United States responsible for an act of sabotage. Though admitting
he had no proof, Fidel chose to blame Yankee imperialism for the destruction. It was "logical," he argued.
They denied Cuba arms, then prevented Cuba from
getting them elsewhere. The following day he used a
funeral for victims of the explosion to warn America,
"You will reduce us neither by war nor famine." With
controlled emotion he promised the huge crowd gathered at the entrance to Colón cemetery, "We shall
answer counter-revolutionary terror with revolutionary terror." [1] Skillfully, Fidel milked the *Coubre*
incident for all its propaganda value to cast the
United States as the enemy bent on destroying the
revolution. He also used it to justify the need for
armaments from the Soviet Union to protect Cuba
from further Yankee aggression.

America denied any connection to the *La Coubre*
explosion. By the spring of 1960, however, it had
committed itself to active support of Cuban exiles
against Castro. President Eisenhower authorized
the CIA to train and equip a force to invade Cuba. In
his speeches, Fidel often warned of such an invasion.
The phrase *Cuba sí, Yanqui no!* became a popular
rallying cry as Fidel whipped up popular support in
defense of the revolution. Swords had been drawn on
both sides, though the first serious clashes were on
the economic, rather than the military, front.

When the first shiploads of Russian crude oil
were on their way to the port of Havana, Fidel deliv-

ered an ultimatum to Standard Oil, Texaco, and Royal Dutch, the major foreign-owned oil refineries based in Cuba: Process the oil or be taken over. The companies refused and were nationalized by the end of June.

The American retaliation was swift. The Eisenhower administration cut the American sugar import quota by 700,000 metric tons. Fidel struck back, apparently against the counsel of his advisers, by nationalizing the American-owned telephone and electric utilities, and most of the remaining oil refineries and sugar mills not already taken over.

Fidel's impulsiveness would prove costly in the long term. The Cuban government was not prepared to run these enterprises efficiently. It didn't. The takeovers clearly demonstrated the extent to which Fidel was in charge, acting the traditional *caudillo* who could make and carry out decisions even when they were clearly wrong. "Communism!" screamed the American government as it cut off military and economic aid to Cuba, then attempted to turn the Organization of American States against the Castro regime.

In this atmosphere of mutual hostility, Fidel made a return visit to the United States on September 18, 1960, to speak before the United Nations. The Eisenhower administration, now in its last days before the election of a new president, was not pleased but could not easily prevent Fidel from exercising his right as the leader of a U.N. member nation. In a fit of pique, it did restrict the Cuban delegation to the confines of New York City. Not to be outdone, Fidel restricted the movement of the American ambassador in Havana to a small district within the city.

In New York, Fidel took every opportunity to denounce U.S. actions, generate international interest in Cuba, and generally embarrass his American hosts. He rejected plans to house his delegation in the Hotel Shelbourne. Too expensive. Perhaps, he told the press, they should all hang hammocks in the U.N. garden. Or maybe camp out in Central Park.

In the end, he settled on the Hotel Teresa in the Harlem ghetto, one of the poorest areas of the city. Cheap, and with a reputation as a bordello, the Teresa was a suitable place for a champion of the downtrodden victims of imperialism. Fidel was great newspaper copy. Articles reported tales of Cuban diplomats slaughtering chickens and stewing them in their hotel rooms. The streets outside the Teresa rang with the shouts of demonstrators, both pro- and anti-Castro. The New York police worked overtime.

Fidel saved his best performance for September 26, in his speech before the United Nations General Assembly. Speaking from memorized notes, he moved from the rational to the emotional and back again for almost five hours—too long for many of the delegates, who nodded off to the sound of the translator's voice. Most of Fidel's speech was a history lecture. He described Cuba as a longtime American "colony" controlled by monopolies that kept men like Batista in power. He berated the United States for opening its doors to Batista's followers—"a gang of murderers who had left our country covered with blood." He characterized the Cuban-American sugar agreement as the kind "made between the shark and the sardine."

He then lashed out at the U.S. government for supplying the bombs and airplanes recently used to attack Cuba from the American mainland. "May I take this opportunity," he intoned dramatically, "to tell His Excellency, the Representative of the United States, that there are many mothers in Cuba still awaiting their telegrams of condolence for their chil-

dren murdered by the bombs of the United States."
This same government, he argued, was now planning
military action against Cuba. It would use the naval
base at Guantánamo to provoke an "incident" justi-
fying an invasion.

Presidential candidate John F. Kennedy came in
for special censure. Fidel called Kennedy "an illiterate and ignorant millionaire," probably in response
to the senator's advocacy of aid to the anti-Castro
exiles. Republican candidate Richard Nixon also
took some barbs. Both he and Kennedy, claimed Fidel, "lacked political brains." [2]

Aside from giving Fidel an opportunity to lash
out at the United States on an international stage,
and to meet personally with Premier Nikita Khrushchev of the Soviet Union, the trip to New York accomplished little. Fidel even lost his plane, which was
impounded by U.S. authorities for nonpayment of
debts. Fidel returned to Havana on September 28
in a borrowed Russian airliner. The economic war
continued.

On October 13, Eisenhower stepped up pressure
on Cuba with a ban on all U.S. exports to the island,
except for some foods and medicine. Again Fidel responded by hitting hard at U.S. investments in Cuba.
In the next several weeks, the government took over
548 private businesses, including U.S. nickle interests, banks, distilleries, movie theaters, and large
stores. Some of the biggest names in private enterprise—Woolworth, General Electric, International
Harvester, Coca Cola—fell like dominoes.

Temperatures rose quickly. Eisenhower recalled
American Ambassador Philip Bonsal on October 29.
Neither he, nor any other American ambassador, has
since returned to Cuba. Fidel told his people that a
Yankee invasion was imminent and ordered a gen-
eral mobilization of troops to protect the country.

He demanded a reduction in the staff of the U.S. Embassy. Eisenhower responded by breaking diplomatic relations with Cuba, an act which at other times and places was the prelude to armed conflict. This was indeed Fidel's interpretation.

In speech after speech, Fidel warned that an attack was now inevitable. In fact, the CIA did have an invasion in the works. Cuban exile forces were being trained in Guatemala. The favored plan was for a brigade-sized force of 1,000 to 1,500 men to arrive by sea and secure a beachhead on the Cuban coast. Air cover would be supplied by American planes with Cuban pilots. A Cuban government-in-exile would follow the successful landing and ask for U.S. assistance. The success of the plan hinged on a popular uprising of the Cuban people in support of the invaders. This would happen, said the CIA, because discontent with Fidel Castro was widespread. It was one of many miscalculations.

Fidel's popularity had never been greater. Toward the end of 1960, the people crowded the Plaza de la Revolución to hear Fidel read yet another declaration. Amid the reading of official documents and the poetry of honored guest Pablo Neruda of Venezuela, the people sang and danced in the usual carnival spirit that seemed to surround Fidel's public appearances. Thousands marched around the plaza chanting, "Fidel, go ahead / Hit the Yankees on the head."

The newly elected president of the United States, John F. Kennedy, inherited the invasion plan from the Eisenhower administration. Though Fidel had earlier labeled candidate Kennedy as an "illiterate and ignorant millionaire," he voiced the hope that the new president would abandon invasion plans for a less "insane" approach. Kennedy's inaugural address on January 20, 1961, seemed to soften the

American position. Fidel responded with a speech of his own on the same day.

> Today the new president spoke. His speech had some positive aspects which we welcome, especially when he tries to make a new approach. . . . It is a difficult task. . . . He will have to choose between yielding to great pressures . . . or deciding bravely to face up to them. We Cubans don't want to prejudge. We can wait calmly. We have no hatred or hysteria.[3]

Actually, Kennedy supported the invasion plan, if reluctantly. What he did not want was any direct involvement by the United States. That word never filtered down to the Cuban insurgents. They expected far more assistance than they would ever receive.

After the first weeks of February it was clear to any keen observer that an assault on Cuba was imminent. Fidel knew it from monitoring U.S. newspaper reports and from the increased CIA activity among counterrevolutionary groups operating in Cuba. Fidel the revolutionary fighter was once again in his element. It was like the old days in the Sierra Maestra, and once again the enemy was his own people supported by the colossus to the north.

In the early morning of April 15, eight American B-26 bombers took off from a field in Nicaragua. Their Cuban pilots hoped to destroy Fidel's small airforce in surprise raids on Havana and Santiago. The mission failed. A few planes were destroyed, but the eight which survived played a key role in neutralizing the invasion force.

The next day, in an emotional speech at a funeral for victims of the air attack, Fidel called the raid another Pearl Harbor, but "twice as treacherous and a thousand times more cowardly." Then, for what-

ever reason, he chose that moment to openly proclaim for the first time that the Cuban revolution
was a socialist movement. In a booming voice he
proclaimed, "What the imperialists can't forgive us
for is having forged a socialist revolution under the
very nose of the United States." [4]

Having disembarked from Nicaragua after being
told by its dictator, Anastasio Somoza, to "get a few
hairs from Fidel's beard," the invaders landed at the
Bay of Pigs, an isolated area of beaches and swamps
on Cuba's south coast. On paper, their situation
looked promising. They had support ships, landing
craft, and air support from the B-26s based in Nicaragua. They were reasonably well trained and had
good equipment furnished by the United States.
They also had American CIA advisers. Certainly the
force was larger and better equipped than Fidel's
had been in 1956.

Two elements were missing, however. The expected popular uprising of unhappy Cubans in opposition to Fidel never materialized. Worse, once the
invasion was launched, the United States offered
no support. The failure of the invasion was almost
guaranteed.

The fighting lasted for several days. Some of it
was fierce. Fidel's little air force pounced on the attackers, sinking transport ships, shooting down B-26
bombers, and harassing the invaders on the beach.

Fidel himself came to the front and supervised
much of the defense. A photo soon circulated worldwide showed him in battle fatigues, rifle in hand,
with the familiar cigar clamped tightly in his teeth.
On the third day of the fighting, a jeep carrying Fidel,
Carlos Franqui, and an escort stopped near the front
lines. Suddenly, an enemy patrol burst out of the
cover nearby, threw down their weapons, and surrendered. "One burst of machine-gun fire," recalled

Franqui, "would have sent the lot of us to the next world."[5] The old Fidel luck was still in place.

Cut off and unsupported, the invaders could only surrender. The Cuban army rounded up the survivors—1,180 of the original 1,297—and took them as prisoners to Havana. Fidel realized their propaganda value. He made sure they were treated well and that the world knew of it. Some appeared on Cuban television, debating with Fidel about their motives and actions. They lost the war and they lost the debate.

The Bay of Pigs was a serious setback and embarrassment for the United States. It was a great personal triumph for Fidel Castro, a slap in the face to Yankee imperialism and a tribute to his leadership of the revolution. It raised his prestige at home and abroad, eliminated the most serious threats to his government, and strengthened his relationship with the Soviet Union, which had promised "all necessary assistance in beating back the armed attack on Cuba." Further, it put Cuba squarely and publicly on the path of Marxist socialism.

The Bay of Pigs, or Playa Girón as the Cubans referred to it, unified the nation behind Fidel. As he described it later, "Our Marxist-Leninist party was really born at Girón; from that date on, socialism became cemented forever with the blood of our workers, peasants, and students."[6]

In the failed Bay of Pigs invasion, Fidel found the perfect excuse to tighten his hold on Cuba by eliminating internal opposition. All opposition, no matter who it came from, was branded as CIA-inspired. In a series of police sweeps, thousands of people were arrested, often under the flimsiest of suspicions. When the jails could hold no more, the government detained suspects in stables, corrals, and sports arenas. Though most were released in several weeks, thousands remained in jail to face charges of counterrevolutionary activity. Fidel's political police, known as G.2, came to be as feared by many Cubans as the old secret police under Batista.

Aside from the police, Fidel used the people themselves as agents of their own repression. He created Committees for the Defense of the Revolution (CDRs), neighborhood security organizations that encouraged people to spy on one another. It was George Orwell's Big Brotherism come to life with a distinctly Fidel twist. Most Cubans, it appears, were willing to suffer a bit of repression for the sake of preserving the revolution and protecting the country from another invasion. They left it up to Fidel, who could do little wrong, even if things were going badly. And they were.

The Cuban economy was a mess. The flow of goods from America had stopped by the middle of 1960. The economic blockade proved devastating in a country accustomed to cars, refrigerators, radios, TVs, electric irons, fans, washing machines, locomotives, merchant ships, and a whole range of foodstuffs, from butter to Coca Cola, that came from the United States. It took a while to feel the pinch, because the stores had been full at the time of the blockade. Soon everything was in short supply.

To make matters worse, the bad decisions, poor planning, waste, inefficiency, and mismanagement of the early years of the revolution had created bills that now had to be paid. The country could barely feed itself anymore. Either because of shortages or the inability to get food to the market, even the basics—rice, beans, eggs, fish, milk—had to be rationed by early 1962. The sugar industry, Cuba's big money-maker, was also in trouble. Poor management practices in 1960–1961 meant Cuba could not harvest enough cane to supply its customers for 1962.

Amidst growing repression, shortages, and disorder, more Cubans, especially those of the middle classes, decided to desert the revolution and try their luck elsewhere. Between 1959 and 1962, some 200,000 Cubans—almost 3 percent of the population—became exiles. Many more would leave in the future.

Because of the sad state of the Cuban economy, and the continued threat of invasion from the United States, Fidel needed the Soviet Union more than ever. He worked hard for closer economic and military ties. That was probably why he made the dramatic announcement of December 1961 that he was a Marxist-Leninist and would be one until he died. He thought it would endear him to the Communist bloc. It was laughable. With a straight face, Fidel might call himself anything he wished, but under the veneer of any label he was always first and foremost a "Fidelist" or "Castroite." He owed allegiance to himself and his own ideas rather than to a cause someone else invented, whether it be Marx, Lenin, or Martí. Fidel embraced communism because it suited his purposes to do so, not because he was a Communist. In Cuba, the Communist party had a strong organization and a coherent plan for building a new social order. He needed both.

Fidel turned to the Soviet Union. America, with its constant nagging about voting and other democratic forms, and with the way its great economic and cultural bulk overshadowed Cuba, had nothing to offer. The Soviets, on the other hand, seemed to offer everything. They would underwrite and defend the revolution and they wouldn't meddle with his control. Khrushchev went out of his way to assure

Fidel that he saw the Cuban revolution as a Castro revolution and would recognize no interest or party (including the Communist party) above his leadership. It was exactly what Fidel wanted to hear.

In July 1960, Fidel despatched his brother Raúl to Moscow to get a promise of greater protection from U.S. invasion and more military hardware to build up Cuba's own forces. There was good reason to believe another invasion might take place. The United States was involved in a secret war against Cuba. Florida-based exiles supported by the CIA landed in Cuba regularly to commit acts of sabotage and aid anti-Castro rebels in the Escambray mountains. The CIA also sponsored attempted assassinations of the Cuban leader. Such acts could certainly be seen as attempts to prepare Cuba for invasion.

In the United States, there was always talk of another invasion. Kennedy was under constant fire by political opponents for "losing Cuba to the Communists" and allowing it to remain Communist. Given the level of hostile acts and threatening chatter in the United States, and given the poor state of the Cuban economy and the potential for unrest at home, Fidel needed some shoring up militarily. When Raúl returned from Moscow, he brought with him commitments of military assistance that would soon bring the world to the brink of nuclear war.

The Soviets promised a wide array of sophisticated and powerful military hardware. Included were surface-to-air missiles (SAMs), jet fighters, bombers capable of delivering nuclear weapons, and four battle groups of ground soldiers with tactical nuclear weapons. Most important, they agreed to send medium range ballistic missiles (MRBMs) capable of carrying nuclear and thermonuclear warheads into the heart of the United States.

Why the Soviets planted missiles in Cuba has

long been a subject for conjecture. Was it Fidel's doing? Perhaps he saw himself as a new player in the Cold War with a chance to become a world leader. Maybe he believed the missiles were the only sure way to prevent a U.S. invasion. Or did Nikita Khrushchev maneuver Cuba into taking the missiles? Perhaps Cuba was just a pawn in a larger game and the missiles a lever by which the United States could be moved out of Berlin. Maybe Khrushchev used Cuba to boost his own prestige in the leadership of the Communist party of the Soviet Union. Whatever their purpose for being there, the missiles constituted a threat to world peace.

In the last week of August 1960, President Kennedy began to learn of the possibility of offensive missiles in Cuba. On August 29, an American high-altitude spy plane, the U-2, spotted SAM installations on the island, defenses usually associated with missile sites. Further U-2 flights confirmed the construction of missile-launching complexes in various areas of Cuba. Kennedy responded aggressively, perhaps more so than either the Cubans or Russians expected.

On October 22, Kennedy informed the world about the presence of Russian missiles in Cuba. He claimed it was an aggressive act that dangerously upset the balance of power. The United States, he made clear, would not shrink from nuclear war if it came to that. Giving teeth to his words, the President ordered a quarantine of Cuba by naval blockade. All Communist-bloc ships suspected of carrying arms to Cuba would be stopped and searched. The blockade went into effect on October 24. Twenty-five Soviet ships were already bound for Cuba. The temperature of the crisis was rising.

Fidel's response to Kennedy was to condemn the U.S. naval action as an act of "piracy" and to mobilize his people for war. Soon, however, the missile crisis became a struggle between the two superpowers. Fidel, to his enormous frustration, found little he could do to influence events. He simply was not consulted. On October 27, the missile crisis came to a head when an American U-2 was shot down over Cuba.

Later Fidel claimed that he, personally, shot down the plane. Carlos Franqui believed this to be true. According to Franqui's account, a Soviet general was taking Fidel on a tour of a missile installation when the U-2 appeared on radar. When Fidel asked how the site would be defended from attacking planes, the general pointed to a button. "This one?" said Fidel, pushing the button and shooting down the plane with a surface-to-air missile. "Well, now we'll see if there's a war or not," commented Fidel.[7] Fidel's claim is dubious. The official Russian explanation, and Khrushchev's own, attributes the downing of the U-2 to the Soviet commander of the missile site.

Kennedy reacted decisively to the destruction of the American plane. He placed all nuclear and conventional forces on alert and readied an invasion force to attack Cuba from Florida. To Khrushchev he reiterated the demand for the immediate withdrawal of missiles and bombers from Cuban soil. In exchange, Kennedy offered a pledge that the United States would not attack Cuba in the future. The deadline for the Russian decision was October 30. For a time America and Russia stood eyeball to eyeball on the edge of nuclear confrontation. Khrushchev, knowing his country faced American nuclear superiority, blinked first. He agreed to withdraw the missiles in exchange for Kennedy's pledge not to attack Cuba. The crisis was over, and Fidel had not been consulted.

Fidel heard the news by telephone while having

a discussion with Che Guevara. He blew up at Khrushchev's effrontery. "Son of a bitch! Bastard!" Fidel kicked the wall, then in his furor smashed a plate glass mirror. His anger over the Soviet betrayal was echoed the next day in *Revolucion*'s front page story headlined "SOVIETS WITHDRAW MISSILES." A new song soon floated through the streets of Havana ridiculing Khrushchev for going back on his promise and urging Fidel once more to "Bop the Yankees on the head."

Fidel seemed willing to push the missile crisis much further than his Soviet partners. In dramatic speeches, he had prepared Cubans to defend the revolution at all costs against America's atomic bombs. "[T]here is little question anymore," Georgie Anne Geyer wrote in *Guerrilla Prince*, "that Castro was perfectly ready . . . to launch a nuclear war against the United States." [8]

Despite his anger over the resolution of the missile crisis, Fidel came out of it well, as he usually did in such situations. True, he had no missiles, but he did have Kennedy's assurance that there would be no U.S. attack on Cuba. The crisis also infused Cubans with a new level of nationalistic fervor and a sense of Cuba-against-the-world. Fidel harnessed these forces to rebuff all demands that a team of U.N. observers should be allowed to inspect the former missile sites. Finally, the superpower confrontation so thoroughly frightened the world about the likelihood of nuclear war that it created some tolerance for the kind of conventional mischief Fidel was creating abroad. No one wanted another missile crisis.

For a time, Fidel's relationship with the Soviets was strained. Then bad feelings gave way to the practical realities of Cuba's economic dependence on the U.S.S.R. All seemed to be forgiven when Fidel flew to Moscow in the spring of 1963. Khrushchev made it clear that nothing was too good for Fidel. For a month he criss-crossed the Soviet Union, cheered and toasted like the guerrilla prince he was. Khrushchev recognized him as a Hero of the Soviet Union, the country's highest honor. Fidel returned to Havana with a renewed fondness for his Communist allies and new strategies for confronting the enemies of the revolution, especially the United States.

In Dallas, Texas, on November 22, 1963, Lee Harvey Oswald shot and killed the president of the United States, John F. Kennedy. In the frenzy of investigation and speculation that followed the assassination, Fidel's name came up often. Many believed he had both the motive and the means to kill the president, charges he vehemently denied. The American CIA had attempted to assassinate Fidel at least seven times, including one plot involving a poisoned milkshake. Had Fidel retaliated? No conclusive proof of a Fidel Castro involvement in the Kennedy assassination has ever come to light.

The 1960s and 1970s were the decades of Fidel's great success as a world leader as he made Cuba a center of revolutionary activity for the Third World. Thousands of men and women came from across the globe—North and South America, Africa, Southeast Asia, the Middle East—to learn the arts of insurrection and guerrilla warfare. Fidel taught them the skills to topple governments and sent them out to serve in his guerrilla empire and turn the world upside down.

In the early 1960s, Cuba-trained guerrilla groups operated in Venezuela, Colombia, Guatemala, El Salvador, Honduras, and Costa Rica. By 1964, Fidel had extended his sphere of influence to Africa. Cuba-trained guerrillas successfully overthrew the government of Zanzibar and established a Marxist state.

Until 1966, when he returned from the Congo-

Brazzaville, Che Guevara was Fidel's agent for revolutionary activity in Africa. Che fell into disfavor because of his loud criticism of Soviet exploitation of Third World countries. In an emotional farewell letter read publicly by Fidel, Che renounced his Cuban citizenship and explained why he was leaving his adopted country. "Other nations of the world call for my modest efforts. I can do that which is denied you because of your responsibility as the head of Cuba and the time has come for us to depart." [9]

Fidel may have had real feelings for the man who had fought so closely by his side for the cause of independence. Yet Che's departure was not what it seemed. Because of his verbal attacks on the Soviets and his poor performance as Minister of Finance, Che had outlived his usefulness to Fidel and the revolution. Fidel fired him.

Saying good-bye to Cuba, Che went to Bolivia to lead a guerrilla force in the building of a new revolution he hoped would sweep through Latin America. Nothing worked. Che was captured by Bolivian soldiers and executed in October 1967. Che Guevara was mourned loudly and publicly in Cuba. There his picture became, and remains, a kind of religious object. As a symbol of the revolutionary ideal, he was of greater value to Fidel dead than alive.

Fidel's adventurism abroad continued strong into the 1970s. There was new Cuban-sponsored guerrilla activity in Chile, Argentina, Uruguay, and Jamaica. But it would be in far-away Angola that Fidel would achieve his greatest success.

In 1975, after centuries of colonial occupation, Portugal granted Angola its independence. Prior to independence day on November 11, there was great jockeying for political position by pro-Western and Marxist groups. Fidel got himself invited to Angola, sent thousands of troops, and ensured that, when morning broke on independence day, the Popular Movement for the Liberation of Angola (MPLA) was firmly in control. Fidel planned for Angola to serve as the center of revolutionary activity in Africa.

From Angola, Cubans moved to prop up one of the most bloodthirsty rulers in modern Africa, Mengistu of Ethiopia. Fidel then turned his attention back to Central America. He closely supported the Sandinista rebels in their overthrow of the Nicaraguan dictator Anastasio Somoza. Carefully monitoring the fighting from Cuba, Fidel supplied arms and advice that aided in the ouster of Somoza on July 19, 1979.

Nicaragua, like Angola, would become a focal point for revolutionary activity. By 1982, Fidel had pumped $194 million in aid to the Sandinista government. He would continue to support them against the American-backed Contra invasion and would use Nicaragua as a conduit for arms shipments to other Marxist groups in Central America.

About the same time as the Sandinista victory in Nicaragua, a more modest Marxist revolution occurred on the tiny Caribbean island of Grenada. Its leader was Maurice Bishop, a longtime Fidel admirer. By the end of 1979, Fidel and the Soviets had readied Grenada to become a launching pad for guerrilla incursions into other Caribbean islands. Fidel's big plans for Grenada went sour in 1983. Maurice Bishop was overthrown and murdered by another Marxist, Bernard Coard. Fidel took the change in stride until the unexpected happened.

The American government under President Ronald Reagan had been watching events in Grenada with growing concern. The Coard coup prodded it to action on October 25, 1983. Eight thousand eight hundred troops of the "U.S.-Caribbean Security Forces" landed on the island, overwhelmed the half-hearted resistance, and established a provisional government. In limited fighting between U.S. and Cuban soldiers, the Cubans suffered twenty-four killed and fifty-seven wounded.

Grenada in 1983 was Fidel Castro's first defeat. It marked the beginning of bad times for his vision of a worldwide guerrilla empire. Serious problems at home and abroad returned Fidel to his island and the isolation from world events he had worked so hard to escape.

CHAPTER SEVEN

THE
REVOLUTION
UNDER
SIEGE

Fidel Castro has always been quick to point out that the Cuban revolution must be seen as more than just another historical event. It is a living, breathing, on-going process of social and political change. Fidel, as the architect and guiding power of that revolution, made many promises to the Cuban people as, together, they labored to build a new society. Some of those promises were kept over the years; many others were not.

The promise Fidel delivered on from the earliest years of the revolution was social improvement for the masses, the common people with whom he most closely identified and those who provided the mainstay of his support. He raised their standard of living, gave them proper medical care, taught them to read and write, educated their children, put them to work, and gave them pride in their country. Fidel did these things for his people, *las masas*, and they loved and trusted him in return. For these accomplishments, Fidel deserves credit. The promises he did not keep, though he says he did, were those of human rights: freedom of movement, freedom of speech, freedom to choose between political alternatives, freedom to know the truth. It may be the case that almost every Cuban can now read and write because of widespread literacy campaigns that became a national priority. It is also true that in Fidel's Cuba the people have little choice about what they may read and must be very careful about what they write.

Cuba is a totalitarian society. The tentacles of state control extend to every facet of life: work, education, the arts, sports, and family. This overmanaged society is the personal creation of Fidel Castro, the man at the top. Despite the appearance of democratically shared power—a constitution, the Communist party, a national assembly and other elected bodies—Fidel dominates the decision-making process. He has largely done so from the beginning, and his power has grown.

The main instrument of Fidel's control is the military, an extension of his old guerrilla army of the Sierra Maestra. Fidel has transformed Cuba into an armed camp. The military is the country's most powerful and important institution. Such developments have been accomplished with widespread public support. Fidel has been an unusually popular dictator, though support has waned in the face of increasingly hard times. If, indeed, the masses turn away from Fidel, it is because there are some problems that even he cannot solve or manipulate to his advantage. Fidel's famous string of luck finally may be running out, and he has brought the situation on himself.

Though not an economist or even much of a director, Fidel has personally directed the Cuban economy through its many ups and downs since 1959. He has made the economy what it is today, a system on the point of collapse. Two of his major political decisions—confronting the United States at every turn and hitching his star to the Soviet Union—have hurt Cuba in the long run. His insistence on personal economic decisions, often against good advice, has resulted in a series of blunders.

Early in the revolution, Fidel had been committed to ending Cuba's overwhelming dependence on sugar and moving to a more diversified economy. At the end of 1961, against expert advice, he told Cubans to destroy part of the cane fields in order to plant vegetables and fruit. In the resulting disorder, the vital cane harvest was reduced by 50 percent. Later, under the influence of Soviet economic advice, he chose to stick with sugar as Cuba's main source of income and worked to raise production. Soviet engineers promised to develop mechanical harvesters to cut the sugarcane, thus both increasing the rate of production and freeing Cuban workers from the backbreaking efforts of cutting by hand. It was easier for Fidel to say yes to sugar than to undertake the painful but necessary process of putting the economy on a reduced-sweets diet.

In another fit of misguided enthusiasm, Fidel created a green belt, a band of agricultural land around Havana, for the production of coffee. Ignoring the advice of experts that the land was unsuitable for such cultivation, Fidel spent millions of dollars on seeds and seedlings that were then planted by hand in a massive work project. The plants died as predicted. The joke that went around at the time was: Now we're going to send Fidel to the United States. If he does there what he did here, the United States is done for.

Fidel took as much interest in livestock as he did in sugar. In the 1980s Fidel became obsessed with cows as the answer to some of Cuba's production problems. So great was this fascination that his friend, the noted Colombian writer Gabriel García Márquez, playfully suggested writing a book about Fidel called *The Dictator of the Cows*. Through genetic engineering, Fidel claimed, he could create a super-cow, a source of such quantities of meat and milk that it would astound the agricultural world. His cross-breeding experiment worked for one generation of cows, producing magnificent specimens like the famous Ubre Blanca (White Udder) which Fidel showed off to visitors with almost fatherly pride. Ultimately, the super-cow plan failed to develop successive generations of stock with superior characteristics. Experts had warned Fidel that this would happen. Blinded by his own egotistical enthusiasm, he ignored their advice. His beloved Ubre Blanca now pastures in a museum, a taxidermic monument to Fidel's grand but mistaken design.

As long as the Soviets were willing to prop up the Cuban economy by paying twice the world market price for sugar, by supplying Cuba with cheap oil, and by infusing massive amounts of direct aid into the island, the future looked rosy. Cuba's sugar paid the bills for Fidel's ambition to be the leader of the Third World, and his military adventurism in Latin America and Africa. These were expensive hobbies. Again, Fidel showed his inclination to go for the flashy short-term gain rather than to plan carefully for the future. He allowed Cuba to become far too dependent on Soviet support—between $4 and $5 billion a year. Like many poorer countries, Cuba has suffered economically as a result of a general economic decline in the world during the past several decades. Then, in the late 1980s, when economic decline accelerated in the U.S.S.R. and other Soviet bloc nations, resulting in the Communist system falling apart, Cuba got dragged down with them. Her lifeblood, Russian petroleum, began to slow as the Soviets demanded payment in hard and stable currency—no more bartering or paying in Cuban pesos. This was disastrous for Cuba. Her hard currency reserves amounted to little more than pocket change. What had once been a river of oil flowing into Cuba through the port of Havana slowed to a trickle. The effects of oil-deprivation became painfully evident.

Since oil turns the wheels of Cuba's utilities, factories, and transportation industry, all have slowed drastically. Cutbacks in electrical power have meant no air conditioning in offices and no night baseball games in a country where baseball is the national passion. The sugar industry on which so much depends has been particularly hard hit, creating a Catch-22. There is insufficient gasoline to fuel the harvesters needed to cut sugarcane; without bringing in the sugar crop, Cuba cannot purchase the oil needed to run the harvesting machines. Under such harsh realities, the quality of life in Cuba has steadily deteriorated.

Rationing is now a way of life as imports dwindle and agricultural products don't reach markets because of transportation cutbacks. Cubans must stand in line for even the basics—bread, eggs, meat, milk, cheese, rice, fruit, fish. Even the famous Cuban cigar is subject to a one-a-week rationing regulation. Shelves in stores are almost empty.

The effects of shortages, rationing, insufficient housing, reduction of government services, and unemployment have had a powerful effect on the Cuban family, traditionally the country's most stable and enduring institution. The divorce rate has risen dramatically, as divorce often seems the most direct way to escape the suffocating problems of family life. The government has tried to respond. Housing shortages have resulted in serious overcrowding. Overcrowding has made privacy between husband and wife almost impossible to achieve in tiny homes and apartments containing multiple families. The government's response has been to provide "love-hotels," where married couples can rent a room for a few hours to provide a little private time for intimacy not available elsewhere. For many Cubans, stopgap measures have not provided enough relief from the current economic hardships.

Hundreds of Cubans have defied government laws against leaving the country and have risked their lives to look for a better life. In July 1991, one of the new boat people, Juan Alfredo Molenillo Grenup, sailed on a raft from Cuba to Florida. The thirty-six-year-old laid-off welder is typical of a new wave of Cuban refugees, part of the near-million who have left Cuba since the revolution began. In an interview, Grenup said

> In March, I travelled to Oriente, and people there told me they had been washing themselves with plain water because there was no soap. I told them it had been three months since we had seen socks in Havana. We laughed and cried together. . . . For three months we had eaten no meat. Without food there was nothing to do but leave.[1]

Fidel's response to the economic crisis has been to call for more sacrifices, more belt-tightening, from the Cuban people. "It is possible," he warned in 1989 during a fit of understatement, "that in the future we will have to keep working and making miracles, with problems in supplies from the socialist area."[2] Hoping to nudge a miracle along, Fidel invented the "zero option," a return to a simpler level of life and technology without oil. He relocated 200,000 people from urban areas to the simpler life of the country, then ordered the training of oxen to replace tractors, idle because of the gas shortage. Recently he purchased 200,000 Chinese-made bicycles to get people around in the absence of buses and cars. Rush hour in Havana, which once looked and sounded like the Indianapolis 500, is now more like a bicycle race.

Some of Cuba's economic problems have been long in the making, the outcome of excessive Soviet-style bureaucracy, mismanagement, and poor planning. Fidel's leadership style has contributed to the mess. His unwillingness to share power, and his insistence on having his fingers in almost every pie, have reduced individual initiative and hampered decision-making at lower levels. Cuban administrators do not want to decide anything without checking with Fidel. Even when he doesn't wish to interfere, he undermines the process. Who wants to make a law, a ruling, or an economic plan when Fidel is likely to step in and change everything?

While Fidel will acknowledge that mistakes have been made, he will rarely own up to them himself. When he does, he uses the opportunity to manipulate public opinion, as he did when offering to resign in a speech announcing the failure of the 1969 sugar harvest. Shouts of "No, no, no" rose in waves from the crowd, which stood behind him as solidly as ever. Once again, Fidel made something out of nothing.

In 1989, Fidel started something called "The Process of the Rectification of Errors," which should have been used, as the name suggests, to correct mistakes. It ended up being a process of finding scapegoats to blame. When not blaming the imperialist countries for Cuba's ills, or the Soviets, or internal enemies, Fidel has railed at and scolded the Cuban people themselves for not living up to the revolution. *They* might weaken in the force of growing problems and difficulties, but *he* would never give up on the revolution. "If they told me that 98 percent of the people did not believe in the revolution, I would carry on fighting," he declared in a 1990 speech.[3] "Social-ism or Death!" is now the militant slogan Fidel uses to end his public appearances.

In Cuba under Fidel, there has been little honest appraisal of problems, and certainly no laying of problems at Fidel's door. If they are concerned with surviving, Cubans do not openly criticize the leader-ship unless it serves Fidel's purpose. Except for a few well-publicized dissidents who feel they have little to lose by speaking out, Cuba is a country where most people are afraid to speak their minds.

Fidel has enveloped Cuba in a stifling political atmosphere. There is no free trade-union movement, no free press, and no encouragement to be open and honest. At the center of Fidel's system of control are his Committees for the Defense of the Revolution (CDR), in place since 1963. CDRs are found in every neighborhood of the country. Over 83 percent of all Cubans over fourteen belong to one. Often, they do important work. CDR members regularly monitor street activity late at night, on the lookout for petty crime. They check the streets themselves for repair, help the elderly, participate in vaccination programs for children, and visit the families of soldiers abroad. They also fulfill a more sinister function. CDRs check for evidence of correct political attitudes in schools, factories, clubs, and homes. Members keep track of one another, reporting on "Opinion Collection Forms" what they overhear from people in the streets, in theaters, and in lines waiting for food. Any Cuban who tells a joke at Fidel's expense, or laughs too loudly at one, may find himself in trouble. CDRs keep track of visitors, especially foreigners, monitor who goes to church and who listens to the U.S. govern-ment's Radio Martí broadcasts. Cubans who don't get a good report from the neighborhood CDR may have difficulty getting a new job, or worse.

Cuba's program of Big Brotherism stems from Fidel's passion for unity, the lack of which, he insists, resulted in the failure of earlier Cuban revolutions. He will not allow this to happen to *his* revolution. The resulting repressive atmosphere promotes conformity and brooks no criticism of the leadership. "At present," observed Argentine journalist Jacobo Timerman, who recently traveled in Cuba, "the boundary that Cubans do not cross is the territory occupied by El Comandante and his regime."[4] If there have been any internal challenges to Fidel's leadership, the world has not heard of them. Yet the Ochoa incident may have been just such a challenge.

General Arnaldo Ochoa had attained prominence in the Cuban army during a nineteen-year career. As commander of the Cuban army in Angola, he had been declared a Hero of the Republic. Fidel had rewarded him accordingly with the highest honors and privileges. In 1989, General Ochoa and several associates were arrested and charged with large-scale drug trafficking. After a highly publicized show trial, a courts martial convicted Ochoa. The government executed him in July 1989. Ochoa's conviction on drug charges may have been a smoke screen to hide an attempted overthrow of Fidel Castro.[5] Or perhaps Fidel merely feared that the popular and charismatic Ochoa could serve as the focus of disaffection for thousands of unhappy soldiers returning from Angola to a depressed country that hardly knew what to do with them. A third possibility is that the Ochoa trial was a cover-up for Fidel's own drug connections, which had been carried on through drug cartels in Colombia and Bolivia since the 1970s.

In return for allowing the drug cartels to move cocaine through Cuba to the United States, Fidel was able to channel arms to revolutionary groups in South America by using the well-developed drug transportation network. In time, the Cuban government went into the drug business on its own, raising hundreds of millions of dollars in much-needed hard currency and striking a blow at the United States.[6]

If Cuba has experienced great changes in the thirty-three years of the revolution, Fidel Castro has remained a constant. True, Fidel is no longer young. The beard is gray. The olive-green uniforms have had to be tailored to accommodate a paunch. He no longer has the cigar habit, for health reasons. But basically it is the same old Fidel, at least the one seen in public. The private Fidel is still largely a mystery, the result of what Tad Szulc has called "the secrecy habit of a lifelong conspirator."

Fidel's mother and father are long dead. Fidelito, his son by Mirta, has, until recently, lived a life in the shadows with his Russian wife and three children. Fidel has his younger brother, Raúl, the second in command. Several other brothers and sisters inhabit the back scenes of political life. Fidel's real family, however, has consisted of the men and women with whom he shared the formative years of the revolution.

Many of his old comrades-in-arms are now dead, including two of his closest friends, René Vallejo and Celia Sánchez. Celia's death by lung cancer in 1980 left a void in Fidel's life. He has had relationships with women over the years following his divorce from Mirta. He has fathered illegitimate children, at least six of whom are known. But no woman has meant more to him than Celia. She had devoted her life to Fidel since the time they first met in 1956 in the Sierra Maestra. As the person who managed all the complex personal details of his life, she was his fixed star, a constant reference point and reality check. Her loss has weighed on him.

Other deaths, difficult to explain, have intruded

on Fidel's peace. Near the time of Celia's passing, Haydée Santamaría shot herself through the head on the twenty-seventh anniversary of the Moncada assault in which she had taken part. Having lost her fiancé and brother in support of Fidel that day, she became a heroine of the revolution. Why suicide, people asked, and why on that special anniversary so important to Fidel? He must have wondered. Several years later, Osvaldo Dorticós, the former Cuban president, also committed suicide. Why? Personal reasons, was the official explanations, yet many Cubans believed the suicides were protests against what Cuba had become under Fidel.

Despite the outgoing man-of-the-people image he so carefully projects to the outside world, Fidel is actually shy and introverted in his private life. No doubt it is lonely at the top for one who finds it hard to share either power or himself with others. Now in his late sixties, he must be contemplating the ends of things. How will he leave the center stage he has occupied most of his adult life? Though Fidel told a reporter that he would like to retire and become "just like everybody else," it is difficult to see him in a rocking chair, much less ever being anything other than his unique self. But he also told the reporter, "Diplomats can retire, everyone can retire. The only ones who can't retire are the revolutionaries." [7]

Whether Fidel retires or dies in office, he will leave one day. What will follow is a huge unknown and the subject of a favorite guessing game at home and abroad. There is no Fidel-number-two waiting in the wings. Brother Raúl is a logical successor. He is both respected and feared. Perhaps as a jest, Fidel has often warned Cubans about Raúl. Should something happen to me, he would tell them, look out for Raúl! Some have suggested that Fidelito, who heads Cuba's nuclear development program, is another possible successor to his father. It is difficult to say because it is difficult to envision a Cuba without Fidel.

There is a fear that Fidel may not go quietly, whenever he goes. The writer Georgie Anne Geyer has been watching Fidel for a long time. Her concern is that an irrational Fidel may strike out once more at the United States. She contends that only Soviet restraint kept him from bombing the Turkey Point nuclear power plant in Florida both after the missile crisis of 1962 and during America's invasion of Grenada in 1983. "I don't have nuclear weapons," he is quoted as saying, "but I can create a nuclear explosion." [8]

Fidel is as feisty as ever, even in the face of diminished prestige abroad, desertion by his strongest allies, and a whole range of problems at home. It may be these things that give him strength. He is usually at his best when challenged by odds that would cause weaker beings to wilt.

The world spotlight was once more on Cuba in the summer of 1991. In the midst of his worst economic crisis ever, Fidel was faced with honoring a long-standing commitment to host the 11th Pan American Games. He was determined that Cuba would not be embarrassed by giving up the Games or offering inadequate facilities. By dint of his iron will and centralized control, he muscled through to completion the sixty-six sports complexes needed for the Games. The cost was tens of millions of dollars, which Cuba could ill afford to spend. But he made it happen. Determined that visitors should see Cuba in the best possible light, he created new neighborhood militias called "rapid action detachments" to keep unruly malcontents in line and squelch any demonstrations before the television cameras.

Laborers working around the clock finished the

facilities on time. The Cuban people took justifiable pride in the accomplishment, but the costs to them were evident. Shiny new vehicles built specially for visitors rocketed past crowds of Cubans waiting for their own shoddy and overcrowded buses to come along. As athletes from the Americas ate well in new cafeterias, Cubans waited in long lines for their daily rations of bread. In the shadow of gleaming new and efficient sports arenas, badly needed housing projects waited for completion.

On the day set for the Games to begin, looming storm clouds threatened to mar the official opening ceremonies. At the last moment the skies cleared and a rainbow appeared dramatically overhead. "One might say a miracle occurred in Havana," Fidel announced with a smile.

Fidel's "miracle" demonstrated to a watching world that the old revolutionary could still pull rabbits out of hats as he had done for so many years. Though he passed this test, others loom large on the horizon. Fidel may soon be the last major dictator in a world that seems bent on democratic reforms. He has vowed to stay the course and keep the socialist movement alive in Cuba against all odds. That he can do so as Cuba falls apart around him seems unlikely. No doubt the greatest test of all he stands for and believes in will come after he is gone. Cuba after Fidel will either become a living monument to his revolutionary ideals or the tombstone of another messiah without scruples.

SOURCE NOTES

CHAPTER ONE

1. Fidel's half-brother and sister by Angel's first marriage were Pedro Emilo and Lidia; by Angel's second wife, Lina, they included Raúl, Emma, Angelita, Juanita, and Ramón.
2. Some accounts make no mention of a divorce and claim that Angel lost his first wife when she died. Many of the details of the Castro family history, including Fidel's early years, are unclear. Fidel likes it that way and has seldom been open about his past.
3. Frei Betto, *Fidel and Religion: Conversations with Frei Betto* (Sydney: Pathfinder Press/Pacific and Asia, 1986), p. 69.
4. Tad Szulc, *Fidel: A Critical Portrait* (New York: William Morrow and Company, 1986), p. 109.
5. Ibid., p. 110.
6. Betto, p. 80.
7. Ibid., p. 79.

8. Ibid., p. 84.
9. Szulc, p. 112.
10. Ibid., p. 115.
11. Quoted in Georgie Anne Geyer, *Guerrilla Prince* (Boston: Little, Brown and Company, 1991), pp. 36–37.
12. Betto, p. 103.
13. Ibid., p. 111.
14. Ibid., p. 110.
15. Geyer, p. 44.

CHAPTER TWO

1. Philip Brenner, et al., eds., *The Cuba Reader: The Making of a Revolutionary Society* (New York: Grove Press, 1989), pp. 30–31.
2. Quoted in Hugh Thomas, *Cuba: The Pursuit of Freedom* (New York: Harper and Row, 1971), p. 810.
3. Carlos Franqui, *Family Portrait with Fidel* (London: Jonathan Cape, 1983), p. 150.
4. Georgie Anne Geyer, *Guerrilla Prince* (Boston: Little, Brown and Company, 1991), p. 49.
5. Herbert Matthews, *Fidel Castro* (New York: Simon and Schuster, 1969), pp. 25–26.
6. Ibid., p. 55.
7. Geyer, p. 82.
8. Quoted in interview by Jules Dubois in Franqui, p. 226.
9. "Castro's Curveball," *Harper's Magazine*, May 1989: 32, 34.
10. Geyer, p. 69.
11. Rolando E. Bonachea and Nelson P. Valdés, eds., *Revolutionary Struggle: 1947–1958* (Cambridge, Mass.: The MIT Press, 1972), p. 132.
12. Frei Betto, *Fidel and Religion: Conversations with Frei Betto* (Sydney: Pathfinder Press/Pacific and Asia, 1986), p. 120.

13. Bonachea and Valdés, pp. 147–149.
14. Quoted in Thomas, p. 827.
15. Quoted in Ibid., pp. 833–834.
16. Betto, p. 130.

CHAPTER THREE

1. Fidel Castro, *History Will Absolve Me* (London: Jonathon Cape, 1968), pp. 9–55.
2. Ibid., pp. 61–62.
3. Ibid., p. 43.
4. Ibid., p. 40.
5. Ibid., p. 104.
6. Quoted in Hugh Thomas, *Cuba: The Pursuit of Freedom* (New York: Harper and Row, 1971), p. 854.
7. Frei Betto, *Fidel and Revolution: Conversations with Frei Betto* (Sydney: Pathfinders Press/Pacific and Asia, 1986), p. 135.
8. Thomas, p. 860.
9. Bonachea and Valdés, p. 257.
10. Ibid., p. 260.
11. Thomas, pp. 872–873.
12. Bonachea and Valdés, p. 282.
13. Ibid., p. 318.
14. Ibid., p. 340.

CHAPTER FOUR

1. Tad Szulc, *Fidel: A Critical Portrait* (New York: William Morrow and Company, 1986), p. 29.
2. Georgie Anne Geyer, *Guerrilla Prince* (Boston: Little, Brown and Company, 1991), pp. 167–168.
3. Hugh Thomas, *Cuba: The Pursuit of Freedom* (New York: Harper and Row, 1971), p. 919.
4. Lee Lockwood, *Castro's Cuba, Cuba's Fidel* (New York: Macmillan Company, 1967), p. 24.

5. Carlos Franqui, *Family Portrait with Fidel* (London: Jonathan Cape, 1983), p. 3.
6. Ibid., pp. 247–248.
7. Rolando E. Bonachea and Nelson P. Valdés, eds., *Revolutionary Struggle: 1947–1958* (Cambridge, Mass.: The MIT Press, 1972), p. 350–351.
8. Franqui, p. 250.
9. Quoted in Daniel James, *Ché Guevara* (New York: Stein and Day, 1969), p. 95.
10. Franqui, p. 8.
11. Ibid., pp. 12–13.

CHAPTER FIVE

1. Carlos Franqui, *Family Portrait with Fidel* (London: Jonathan Cape, 1983), p. 8.
2. Thomas, p. 1087.
3. Lee Lockwood, *Castro's Cuba, Cuba's Fidel* (New York: Macmillan Company, 1967), p. 177.
4. Carlos Franqui in *Family Portrait with Fidel* claimed that "in Washington the prevailing atmosphere was pure disdain." (p. 32) In *Guerrilla Prince* (p. 233), Georgie Anne Geyer says that the State Department's treatment of Castro was cordial though he may have felt miffed because President Eisenhower did not make himself available.
5. Quoted in Franqui, p. 230.
6. Maitland A. Edey, editor, *Time Capsule/1959* (New York: Time Life Books, 1968), pp. 94–95.
7. Geyer, p. 235.
8. Richard M. Nixon, *The Memoirs of Richard Nixon* (New York: Grosset and Dunlap, 1978), p. 202.
9. Franqui, p. 37.
10. Ibid., p. 149.
11. Ibid., pp. 232–233.
12. Tad Szulc, *Fidel: A Critical Portrait* (New York: William Morrow and Company, 1986), p. 504.

CHAPTER SIX

1. Quoted in Carlos Franqui, *Family Portrait with Fidel* (London: Jonathan Cape, 1983), p. 70.
2. Martin Kenner and James Petras, eds., *Fidel Castro Speaks* (New York: Grove Press, 1969), pp. 3–36.
3. Quoted in Maurice Halperin, *The Rise and Decline of Fidel Castro* (Berkeley: University of California Press, 1972), p. 92.
4. Tad Szulc, *Fidel: A Critical Portrait* (New York: William Morrow and Company, 1986), p. 547.
5. Franqui, p. 125.
6. Quoted in Szulc, p. 556.
7. Franqui, p. 193.
8. Georgie Anne Geyer, *Guerrilla Prince* (Boston: Little, Brown and Company, 1991), p. 292.
9. Quoted in Geyer, p. 310.

CHAPTER SEVEN

1. "Refugees describe Cuba's privation," *Milwaukee Journal*, 4 Aug. 1991.
2. *Latinamerican Press*, 25 Jan. 1990.
3. "Cuban evolution: Castro toys with modest reforms," *Milwaukee Journal*, 17 March 1991.
4. Jacobo Timerman, *Cuba: A Journey* (New York: Alfred A. Knopf, 1990), p. 75.
5. Ibid., p. 82.
6. John Barron, "Castro, Cocaine and the A-Bomb Connection," *Reader's Digest*, March 1990.
7. Eugene Robinson, "Castro: Let World Change, Cuba Will Stay the Course," *Washington Post*, 17 March 1990.
8. Georgie Anne Geyer, "Is Castro near his final act?", *The Detroit News*, 28 July 1991.

FOR FURTHER READING

Betto, Frei. *Fidel and Religion: Conversations with Frei Betto*. Sydney: Pathfinder Press, 1986.

Bonachea, Rolando E. and Nelson P. Valdés, eds. *Revolutionary Struggle 1947–1958:* Volume 1 of the *Selected Works of Fidel Castro*. Cambridge, Mass.: The MIT Press, 1972.

Bourne, Peter G. *Fidel: A Biography of Fidel Castro*. New York: Dodd, Mead and Co., 1986.

Brenner, Philip, William M. LeoGrande, Donna Rich, and Daniel Siegal, eds. *The Cuba Reader: The Making of a Revolutionary Society*. New York: Grove Press, 1989.

Draper, Theodore. *Castroism: Theory and Practice*. New York: Frederick A. Praeger, 1965.

Franqui, Carlos. *Family Portrait with Fidel*. Trans. Alfred MacAdam. London: Jonathon Cape, 1983.

Geyer, Georgie Anne. *Guerrilla Prince: The Untold Story of Fidel Castro*. Boston: Little, Brown and Co., 1991.

Guevara, Ernesto "Che." *Reminiscences of the Cuban*

Revolutionary War. Trans. Victoria Ortiz. New York: Monthly Review Press, 1968.

Halperin, Maurice. *The Rise and Decline of Fidel Castro*. Berkeley: University of California Press, 1972.

Kenner, Martin and James Petras, eds. *Fidel Castro Speaks*. New York: Grove Press, Inc., 1969.

Lockwood, Lee. *Castro's Cuba, Cuba's Fidel*. New York: Macmillan Co., 1967.

Montaner, Carlos Alberto. "The Roots of Anti-Americanism in Cuba." *Caribbean Review*, Spring 1984: 13–16, 42–46.

Szulc, Tad. *Fidel: A Critical Portrait*. New York: William Morrow and Co., Inc., 1986.

Thomas, Hugh. *Cuba: The Pursuit of Freedom*. New York: Harper and Row, 1971.

Timerman, Jacobo. *Cuba: A Journey*. Trans. Toby Talbot. New York: Alfred A. Knopf, 1990.

Vier, Gene. "Analyzing Fidel." *Human Behavior*, July 1975: 64–71.

INDEX